The Banker's Art

永泉泰

憑票發當拾銅元壹伯枚整

字第

號

年　月　日

不抖失票
更換洋板

票

The Banker's Art

STUDIES IN PAPER MONEY

EDITED BY

Virginia Hewitt

PUBLISHED FOR THE TRUSTEES OF
THE BRITISH MUSEUM BY
British Museum Press

© 1995 The Trustees of the British Museum
Published by British Museum Press
A division of The British Museum Company Ltd
46 Bloomsbury Street, London WC1B 3QQ

First published 1995

British Library Cataloguing in Publication Data
A catalogue record for this book is available from the British Library

ISBN 0-7141-0879-0

Designed by Simon Bell

Typeset in Walbaum

Printed and bound in Great Britain by Henry Ling, The Dorset Press, Dorchester

Contents

PART TWO

MAKING PAPER MONEY – DESIGN AND SYMBOLISM

Acknowledgements

These papers were first presented at a conference held in the British Museum in May 1994, to mark the tercentenary of the Bank of England later that year. The enthusiastic response of those who attended and their clear wish for the papers to be published have been a major incentive in the production of this volume, which is the result of the collaboration of many people.

On behalf of all the contributors I would like to thank my colleagues at British Museum Press, especially Emma Way, Teresa Francis, Colin Grant and Julie Young, who have been unfailingly patient and encouraging. Anne Marriott provided valuable editorial assistance, and Simon Bell designed the cover and layouts of text and illustrations. We are also grateful to Douglas B. Ball, Trevor Jones of Banking Memorabilia, and Pam West of West Promotions, who generously contributed financial support towards the colour plates.

On my own account I wish to thank with affection my friends and family, especially my parents, for their interest in the project and their tolerance of my immersion in it. Robert Heslip not only compiled the index, but has also cheerfully provided perspective and good humour whenever needed. I am also grateful to John Keyworth at the Bank of England for giving helpful advice at very short notice. My colleagues here at the Department of Coins and Medals have, as ever, given support which is always welcome and never taken for granted; my thanks go particularly to Andrew Burnett, Barrie Cook, Janet Larkin and Luke Syson, and to Margaret Massey and Beverley Fryer who produced the typescript with their usual impressive speed and skill. Helen Wang and Joe Cribb have helped in various capacities, as friends, colleagues and contributors.

And it is to my fellow-authors that my final and greatest thanks are due. Faced with alarming deadlines and endless questions, they have responded with charm and courtesy. This book is the product of their commitment, and it has been a pleasure and a privilege to work with them.

Virginia Hewitt

Introduction

Virginia Hewitt

This book has its origins in a conference to mark the 300th anniversary of the Bank of England, but its title pre-dates even that venerable institution by more than a century. In 1572 Dr Thomas Wilson published a *Discourse uppon Usurye* in which he divided the 'bankers art' into the dual skills of exchanging cash and arranging credit, two basic functions through which the history of banking has evolved. The articles presented here focus on another aspect, the creation of paper currency, yet Wilson's early definition, applied to a fledgling profession, remains appropriate. Writing before the foundation of Europe's first note-issuing bank, he reminds us that this art may be practised not only by banks but also by governments, political factions and even individuals. Furthermore, his words carry several pertinent resonances, suggesting both the skill involved in issuing paper money and the visual art in its design and appearance.

The contributors were invited to choose their own subjects in order to reflect their current areas of research: the result was a series of papers whose diversity of subject and approach illustrate the many ways in which banking and paper money may be studied. They are arranged here in two broad themes: firstly, the creation and issue of paper money and, secondly, its manufacture, design and symbolism.

The first three papers look at the role of banks and governments in supplying and controlling a nation's currency. Wiséhn charts the vicissitudes of Europe's first note-issuing bank, Ball suggests that the United States borrowed from the mixed experiences of banking in Britain and Jacobi describes how paper may offer hard-pressed governments an expedient alternative to coin. The next two articles move into more maverick circles to show that issuing money is not always undertaken simply in order to provide a circulating currency. Garami's account of an abortive note issue by an exiled Hungarian revolutionary reveals the power of political motivation and high ideals, which assume a more sinister cast in Bower's two tales of forgery sanctioned by statesmen or practised by conspirators, and intended either way to bring down governments. Much of Bower's work is based on the forged notes themselves, their paper and printing, but, as Cribb shows, these physical properties may be just as valuable for detective work in unravelling a complex sequence of genuine note issues when other evidence is scarce. His process of classification of Hong Kong notes, drawn from an analysis of printing changes, is an effective bridge to the second section, which looks at the techniques of manufacture and the significance of note design.

The first three papers in this section look particularly at the work of printing

The architect Eliel Saarinen, who also designed a
series of Finnish banknotes (see Chapter 12).
(Photo: Museum of Finnish Architecture, Helsinki)

firms. Greenland and Tortella focus on the importance of British technology, though
with different points of emphasis: Greenland describes an innovative process of colour
printing in the nineteenth century, showing that banknote production both inspired
and adapted general developments in printing, while Tortella looks at the influence of
British printers on the content of Spanish note designs, and how political circumstances could affect the choice of printing firm. Wang presents a detailed study of a
small group of notes printed in Shanghai, all designed by the same artist, and shows
how they combine the influence of foreign (western) imagery and traditional Chinese
perspective and symbolism. Once again, as with Bower and Cribb, the survival of the
material gives us insights not just into the objects themselves but into the culture
which produced them.

The last five papers explore the symbolic content of designs on paper money and
how these may reflect the prevailing views of issuing authorities and the general
public. In describing the rosy scenes on early United States local issues, Doty shows
how the dominant class comfortably romanticised the rest of society, but as Swanson
demonstrates in his study of Confederate issues during the Civil War, imagery on notes
might also be used as propaganda for patriotic and political unity. The association
between national note issues and national values continues in Talvio's analysis of the
philosophy behind an architect's striking note designs for the Bank of Finland.
However, as Chavez reveals in a lively gypsy legend, what an image is meant to be
and what the public think they see are not necessarily the same thing. Finally, my own
paper surveys one popular element in note designs – the portrayal of women – and
suggests how this may convey both intended messages and inherited assumptions.

Each of these papers stands as a self-contained study in its own right, but taken
together they reveal several key themes in the study of paper money, recurring across

Engraving by Robert Savage in the American Bank Note Company files under the title 'The Ideal Head of an Algerian Girl'. This vignette appeared on the Bank of Mexico 5 peso note from 1925 to 1972, and was colloquially known as 'the Gypsy' (see Chapter 13).

boundaries of time and place, and manifested in parallel or contrasting experiences. Everywhere we see the influence of external circumstances beyond the development of banking, from economic chaos brought by war and civil unrest to artistic potential offered by innovations in printing technology. The ubiquitous designs of British engravers and printers are discussed in several contexts, though not always with the same conclusion: it is interesting, for example, that just as Spain turned back to British firms for her note production, Finland abandoned them in favour of Finnish firms. Wherever paper money was produced, it was also copied: forgery is therefore a spectre drifting through every article, threatening financial disaster to governments, or capture and punishment to the perpetrators. Indeed the banker's art is repeatedly shown to be a decidedly risky business, with more than one practitioner, however well-intentioned, facing exile or even death in the attempt to contribute to his country's wealth. And therein lies another universally relevant theme: the role of paper money in the contribution to national strength and identity, politically and economically through the creation of banks and other issuers, or symbolically through the significance of the imagery on paper money.

But these are not just accounts of money and institutions, of banks and printing firms, state treasuries and governments. Directly or indirectly, the main theme in each paper is always related to people: the people who issued notes, the people who used them and how people have been depicted on them. The existence of every issue of paper money relies on the initiative of individuals – bankers or merchants, politicians or revolutionaries, artists and inventors – and the success of every issue depends on its use and acceptance by ordinary citizens in their daily lives. It is easy in historical research to lose the immediacy of this personal dimension, but these papers are vivid evidence that studies in the banker's art are also, inevitably, studies in human lives.

1

Sweden's Stockholm Banco and the first European banknotes

Ian Wiséhn

On 30 November 1656 Johan Palmstruch was granted a royal privilege to found a bank in Stockholm. In the same year Queen Christina of Sweden, daughter of the warrior king Gustavus Adolphus, became a convert to Catholicism and consequently abdicated to retire to Rome. She was succeeded briefly by her cousin Charles X Gustavus. The country had been impoverished by Christina's extravagance, and the new king was also faced with enormous debts arising from the recently ended Thirty Years' War (1618–48). To make financial matters worse, the country was soon embroiled in further wars. Charles attacked Poland in 1655 and with the help of Brandenburg crushed the forces of the Polish king in Warsaw in 1656. He then went to war with Denmark, extorting peace by the Treaty of Roskilde in 1658, although hostilities were renewed later that year. Charles X Gustavus died suddenly at Gothenburg and was succeeded by his infant son Charles XI (1660–97). Since the latter was only four when he came to the throne, government was placed in the hands of the widowed Queen and five of her ministers. In 1660 the regency negotiated a peace treaty with Poland, the Holy Roman Emperor and Brandenburg, which led to all the territory wrested from Denmark having to be given back. As a result of these prolonged wars the Swedish economy was in disorder and the copper currency rapidly depreciated. Such was the situation when the new bank was founded.

Johan Palmstruch was born on 13 July 1611 in Riga, Livonia, which at that time was a Swedish possession. It has long been believed that his family was of Dutch origin, but recent research has shown that they were probably from Livonia.

Palmstruch was originally called Wittmacher, but changed his name when he was ennobled in 1651. As a young man, Wittmacher-Palmstruch moved to Holland and in 1635 became a citizen of Amsterdam but in 1639 he was arrested in that city and had to spend years in prison, his creditors declaring that he was insolvent and that they feared he might escape without paying his debts. After his release, however, Palmstruch asserted energetically that he had in fact always possessed large assets in Holland. If this was true, then factors other than insolvency must have been the real reasons for his being detained. As in later years he was constantly referring to the Bank of Amsterdam as a precedent, a plausible hypothesis might be that he was arrested for committing economic espionage.

Plans for founding a bank in Sweden were put forward several times during the first half of the seventeenth century, but these proposals never materialised. For a model, the Swedes looked towards other early European banks. The Banco de Rialto in Venice, established by Acts of the Venetian Senate in 1584 and 1587, appears to have been the first public bank in that city and indeed in Europe. Later, by the Act of 3 May 1619, the Senate established a second public bank known as the Banco Giro, or Banco del Giro, which ultimately became the only public bank of Venice, for generations famous throughout Europe as the Bank of Venice.

The name of the bank set up in Sweden by Palmstruch was Stockholm Banco (Bank of Stockholm), but it is often called the Palmstruch Bank (fig. 1). Its premises were in a house in Stockholm, near the Royal Palace, belonging to the heirs of Field Marshal Count Herman Wrangel, and it seems to have started its business activities in July 1657. The Bank also had branches in Gothenburg, Åbo (Turku) in Finland, and at the coppermines in Falun. Formally, and in accordance with the banking privileges granted to Palmstruch, the Bank was a private enterprise, but through various measures taken by the government it acquired a character not unlike that of a government office. Thus Palmstruch received Royal Letters of Appointment as the Director of the Bank, with the promise of an annual salary. It was further ordained that one half of the net profits of the Bank were to be delivered to the Crown. The Chancellor of the Exchequer was appointed the Bank's Chief Inspector. All the customs revenues, which constituted a short-term fund, were to be paid through the Bank which was consequently included in the administration of the finances of the realm. Another possible way of raising finance was to borrow from the public by way of the Loan Department – Lehnbanco or Länebanco – which also offered loans on a higher interest basis.

During its first years, the Bank was undoubtedly very successful, but clearly with hindsight it made loans rather too liberally – paying out the sums granted in the form of *kreditivsedlar*, or 'credit notes' – and thus found itself heading for insolvency after only a few years. Palmstruch later intimated that he had sometimes felt more or less compelled to grant credit on a rather too extensive scale in order to oblige prominent members of society. The situation first grew critical in the autumn of 1663, when the Bank's cash-in-hand was reduced to a trifling amount. The Bank had become unable to redeem its own credit notes, or even to honour cheques drawn by the authorities on their credit accounts. In October 1663 the government appointed a commission to inquire into the current state of the Bank. This commission suggested that the Bank should call in its own loans in order to redeem its credit notes. A new commission of investigation was appointed in November 1664, the work of which was not finished until March 1667. The Bank's book-keeping, this commission reported, had been very careless, and a considerable cash deficit was brought to light. Palmstruch was held personally responsible for the Bank's losses. On the recommendation of the commission, he was brought before the courts and sentenced to make good to the Crown all losses caused through his administration of the Bank. Indeed, he was subsequently sentenced to death but seven months later the government commuted the death sentence, and in March 1670 he was released from prison. Palmstruch died in February 1671, not quite a year after his release. His tombstone and funeral escutcheon are still to be seen in the parish church of Täby, about twenty kilometres north of Stockholm. No portrait of him is known.

The circumstances that induced the Stockholm Banco to issue banknotes of credit were connected with the currency depreciation of 1660. At this time other forms of paper money were in circulation: interest-free deposit accounts from the Exchange Department, cashier notes and promissory notes. The reason for this was the great weight of the main Swedish currency, the unique *kopparplätmynt*, or copper plate money (fig. 2). This system was not, as has sometimes been represented in other countries, an emergency means of payment, but one with its value strictly reflecting the copper content of the rectangular plates. Copper plate money was introduced in 1644. Plates for the denomination of 10 dalers silver money were struck in copper, each measuring about 30 × 70 cm and weighing nearly 20 kg (rather more than 40 lb): in other words the plate money was extremely unwieldy and rendered payments of large sums of money troublesome, to say the least. Much of the copper plate money was deposited by customers in vaults of the Stockholm Banco. In 1660 the plates depreciated and new plate money was manufactured with a weight of about 83% of the old plates, counted per daler silver money, which was the basic currency. The customers rushed to the Bank to claim their old plate money, which they could now export or melt down with profit as a pure copper metal. Palmstruch, seeing before him the Stockholm Banco without any assets, put forward a plan for issuing official banknotes, which he had already recommended in 1652, suggesting the issue of *kreditivsedlar*, or credit notes, for a transition period. The new banknotes were Palmstruch's own invention, although he asserted in 1664 that they were designed on the model of the so-called *kopparsedlar*, or copper notes, issued by Bergslaget, the great Swedish copper concern: as coinage was scarce, these were given to the miners as receipts for consignments of raw copper. The copper notes could then change hands and be used as money.

Palmstruch did not want to introduce the credit notes on his own authority, but discussed this measure with members of the government. A draft Royal Decree was drawn up empowering the Bank to issue credit notes with a view to facilitating payments. The credit notes were to be legal tender. They were not to be issued to persons other than those who had cash deposited with the Bank. They were to be issued in four currencies – ducats, riksdalers specie, dalers silver money and dalers copper money – and each currency in different denominations, from 100 to 1,000. These various specifications were not printed on the notes, however; details of the currencies and denominations were handwritten. This was for the very practical reason that there were nineteen denominations for each of the currencies, making a total of seventy-six possible different denominations! The credit notes were to be signed by Palmstruch as well as by four employees of the Bank, and the seal of the Bank was to be impressed on them. It is noteworthy that the draft decree already warned the public against counterfeit credit notes, and it was proposed that a counterfeiter of credit notes should be punished in the same way as a counterfeiter of coins. When this draft came up in the Royal Council, however, it was decided that it would be better if the credit notes were to circulate, as the Chancellor said, *natura sua*, or without any compulsion. No-one was obliged to accept the new notes, except the tax-collector. In other words, the government looked on the banknotes as legal tender, although there was no official public announcement to this effect. In practice, too, credit notes were issued also to persons other than depositors, since loans agreed by the Bank were paid out in the form of credit notes. Many of the proposed denominations, incidentally, were never issued.

The first notes, issued in 1661, were denominated in daler copper coinage. They were probably printed forms with handwritten denominations, with the exception of 12½, 25 and 50 daler kopparmynt, which are likely to have had printed denominations. No surviving notes are known. There was also an issue in 1661 of notes in daler silver coinage, but again none have survived. These notes were on printed forms in denominations of round amounts and, as the bearer was not named, they were not assigned or made payable to any particular person or institution. They were guaranteed by an institution having the status of a central bank, and possession of a note was sufficient to constitute a claim on the bank.

The notes issued from 1662 to 1664 were made of thick, white, good quality handmade paper from Uddby Paper Mills near Stockholm, mostly without watermarks, though a few did bear the mill's watermark. The front has black printing, handwritten number and date, and printed denomination together with five handwritten signatures (fig. 3). The Bank's seal is impressed on a separate square of paper, fixed between the signatures (fig. 4). On the back there is a handwritten number and denomination.

The 1666 issue, called *Palmstruchers*, is the best known. These notes were also made of thick, white, handmade paper from Uddby Paper Mills, with a small watermark 'BANCO' within a frame. The front is printed in black, probably at Ignatius Meurer's printing office in Stockholm. The banknote has a figured frame and printed denomination, but handwritten number and date. There are eight handwritten signatures together with impressions of personal seals. Impressions of the seal of the Stockholm Banco appear in three different sizes between the signatures and in front of the number (fig. 5). On the back of the banknote there is a handwritten number, denomination and signature. There are also wafers of paper to give protection at the back of the impressions, except on the uppermost seal (fig. 6). The notes were issued in paper envelopes of which only one has been preserved. Sometimes minor deviations appear in the printing, but from the very beginning the Bank was trying to protect its notes against forgers: this was the world's first banknote with a specific watermark.

The 100 daler silvermynt was issued in January 1666, the 50 daler silvermynt in February 1666, the 25 daler silvermynt in March 1666 and the 10 daler silvermynt in April and May 1666. Only a few banknotes of the 1666 issue are still in existence:

100 daler silvermynt	26 examples known
50 daler silvermynt	8 examples known
25 daler silvermynt	15 examples known
10 daler silvermynt	46 examples known

In October 1667, transfer notes were issued to specific persons who could transfer the note to a second person or to the Bank for redemption. The denomination was 100 daler silver money in copper coins. They were made of white, handmade writing-paper from Uppsala Paper Mills, with the watermark of the mill (a large coat of arms). The transfer notes were folded to create four pages. The first page carried black printing with handwritten number, name and date. Four signatures surrounded the seals of the Stockholm Banco, impressed on a separate square of paper and glued to the note. Further down were six pre-printed transfer texts (fig. 7). The second and third pages each carried eleven pre-printed transfer texts, while the fourth page was blank. On surviving notes several of the transfers are filled in with handwritten names and dates, and have seals (in accordance with the directions on the note).

In the words of Professor Eli Heckscher, the Swedish economist and historian, the invention of credit notes 'constitutes Palmstruch's claim to a place in the history of money and banking'. True, there had existed paper means of payment long before Palmstruch's invention, but the credit notes issued by the Stockholm Banco are the first that may be considered banknotes in the modern sense of the word. These notes are fully comparable to the banknotes of our time. They were on printed paper forms, in round denominations and without specifying a depositor or deposition or any interest demand. The notes were guaranteed by an institution having the status of a central bank and were payable simply to bearer. Possession of a note was sufficient to constitute a claim on the bank at any time. However, the issue of credit notes by the Stockholm Banco was to be no more than a brief episode, while the notes issued some thirty years later by the Bank of England had an infinitely greater influence on future developments.

The Stockholm Banco issued many credit notes on the security of doubtful pledges for loans and found itself insolvent in 1664: it was liquidated in 1668. The bankruptcy was expected by the authorities. However, during the parliamentary session of 1668, a majority of the members were of the opinion that banking activity in Sweden should be continued. It seems to have been generally believed that it was the issue of credit notes that had brought about the downfall of the Stockholm Banco. A new bank, Rikets Ständers Bank (Bank of the Estates of the Realm), now called Sveriges Riksbank (Bank of Sweden), was founded in September 1668. The constitutional status of the bank was unique inasmuch as it was placed under the guaranty and administration of Parliament. It was an entirely new bank and was in no respect a continuation of the Stockholm Banco.

After the difficulties with credit notes, any issue of such notes was prohibited and thus the official forms of the Bank of Sweden went into public circulation as had been the case with the Stockholm Banco. Contrary to the notes of credit, these were not legal tender but they did in practice come to be used to draw money or pay debts in the Bank, in spite of many restrictions. These banknote substitutes were widely used with the result that the Bank of Sweden was forced to offer transfer notes to the public from 1701 onwards, as a sort of legal currency. At first the depositor had to sign the note as did future holders but, as time went by, this was deemed unnecessary, and the transfer notes became more popular and increasingly similar to modern banknotes. These, however, were not issued until 1803, almost 150 years after the Stockholm Banco had brought non-assigned banknotes into circulation.

Bibliography

BRISMAN, S., 'Den palmstruchska banken och riksens ständers bank under den karolinska tiden', in *Sveriges riksbank 1668–1918*, I, Stockholm 1918.

HECKSCHER, E.F., 'The Bank of Sweden in its connection with the Bank of Amsterdam', in J.G. van Dillen (ed.), *History of the Principal Public Banks*, The Hague 1934.

LAGERQVIST, L.O., 'The first European banknotes: the Swedish beginning in the 1660s', in *Rivista Italiana di Numismatica e Scienze Affini*, XCV, 1994, pp. 669–77.

LAGERQVIST, L.O. AND NATHORST-BÖÖS, E., *Sedlar*, Stockholm 1971.

LINDGREN, T., *Riksbankens Sedelhistoria 1668–1968*, Stockholm 1968.

LÖFSTRÖM, K., 'Den palmstruchska banken. Till 250-årsjubiléeti år', in *Bancoposten*, 1918, no. 1, Stockholm 1918.

MONTELIUS, O., 'Historisk öfversikt. Bidrag till de svenska sedlarnas historia', in H. Hildebrand, *Sedelsamlingen i riksbankens myntkabinett*, Stockholm 1915.

PLATBARZDIS, A., 'Sveriges bankväsen 300 år', in *Bancoposten*, 1956, no. 3, pp. 43ff.

PLATBARZDIS, A., 'Europas första sedlar. I-II', in *Bankvarlden*, 1956, pp. 8–9.

PLATBARZDIS, A., *Sveriges Forsta Banksedlar*, Stockholm 1960.

PLATBARZDIS, A., *Sveriges Sedlar*, I, Lund 1963.

WALLÉN, L., *Sveriges Sedlar*, I-II, Stockholm 1984.

WALLÉN, L., 'The first bank-note printers of Sweden – and the basis', in *LLt. Festskrift till Lars O. Lagerqvist*, Numismatiska Meddelanden XXXVII, Svenska Numismatiska Föreningen, Stockholm 1989.

All photographs in this chapter are by RIK-foto, Stockholm

1 (*above*) The large and small seals of the Stockholm Banco.

2 (*right*) 10 daler silvermynt, 1644, from the reign of Queen Christina: Swedish plate money weighing 19.7 kg. (Illustration greatly reduced)

5 (*above left*) Credit note from 1666. The denomination is 10 daler silvermynt (issued in daler silver coinage).

6 (*above right*) The back of a credit note from 1666.

7 (*right*) First page of a transfer note from 1667, issued to a specific person who could transfer the note to another person or to the bank for redemption.

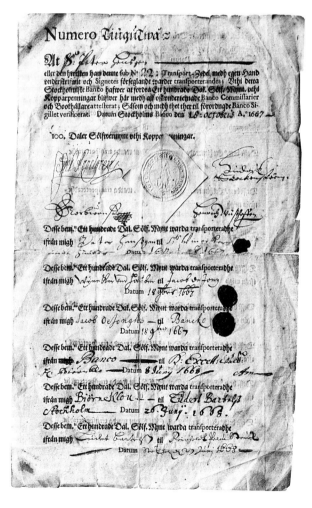

3 (*left*) Credit note from 1662. The denomination is 5 daler kopparmynt (issued in daler copper coinage).

4 (*below*) Impression of the large seal used on the 1662–4 note issues.

2

The influence of the Bank of England and the Scottish banks on American banking, 1781–1913

Douglas B. Ball

Professor Galbraith once noted that while people have attacked Britain's values and even gone to war against them, few in the nineteenth century dared to disparage Britain's financial acumen or the Bank of England. In this paper I want to examine the influence of British banking, both that of the Bank of England and of the Scottish banks, on American banking practices from 1781 to 1913. Without such an understanding, many aspects of American banknote issue will remain obscure.

The relationship began in the 1740s when the British Parliament extended the Bubble Act to the American colonies, prohibiting the formation of any company unless it was incorporated by Royal Charter or Act of Parliament. British traders were adamantly opposed to the various land and manufactory banks proposed by the New Englanders and, by the same token, there was strong opposition in Great Britain to the Americans' shameless resort to a series of inadequately backed paper money issues in practically all the colonies. The last thing the British wanted was to be paid off in a currency nominally worth but 75% of sterling and, in practical terms, often worth as little as 7–14%.

The Bank of England, which had been in existence for nearly a century before the Americans began to experiment with government-related banks, provided a model which both positively and negatively influenced American practice. The same was true of the Scottish banks.

Between the Bank of England and the British government there was, to begin with, a necessary close working relationship. The Bank was to furnish the hard-pressed regime of William and Mary with an urgently needed loan of £1,200,000 (on which a return of 8% was guaranteed) in exchange for a Royal Charter and various corporate banking privileges. It was to hold the government's funds, advance further loans, circulate government exchequer bills (though in practice it also issued its own notes), and function as a normal commercial bank. From 1708 until 1826 the Bank also enjoyed a monopoly of joint-stock banking in England, other note-issuing banks being limited by law to only six partners or less.

As the Bank grew in power and influence after 1722, however, the circulation of government notes faded away. Instead, the end of the eighteenth century saw the Bank providing a circulating medium with notes denominated £5 or higher, except during periods of suspension when notes could not be exchanged for coin and £1 notes were issued. The Bank also performed the functions of a modern commercial bank, taking deposits and making loans to persons other than the government. These activities were continued until the 1930s when the Bank deliberately moved away from commercial business and increasingly assumed the role of a central bank.

Following a major commercial crisis in 1825, an Act in May 1826 permitted banks with more than six partners to operate beyond a sixty-five mile radius of London. The Bank of England therefore retained a monopoly of note issue within this area and was also now permitted to compete with provincial banks by establishing note-issuing branches, the first of which was opened in Gloucester in 1826. An inducement of lower discount rates was offered to local private banks who agreed to forgo their own note issues and handle Bank of England notes. Another effect of the 1825 crisis was a renewed drain on the Bank's gold reserves, in consequence of which the Bank reissued a providential supply of £1 notes left over from the earlier suspension of cash payments from 1797 to 1821.

Developments in Scotland might also provide a role model for American banking. By the early eighteenth century Scotland had two major banking institutions – the Bank of Scotland, founded in 1695, and the Royal Bank of Scotland, founded in 1727 – although the country did not possess anything like the wealth of England. Such bullion as reached Edinburgh had to be carefully hoarded to meet payments abroad, whether in London or further afield. Long before Lord Keynes or the Bretton Woods Conference, the Scots had become adept practitioners of what later became known as the Gold Exchange Standard. An indispensable part of such a system was the substitution of paper for coin. Hence the presence in the mid-eighteenth century of notes denominated under a pound, even as low as an English shilling. The Americans, facing similar problems, took a leaf from the Scots' book – though they might have taken heed of the warning when in 1765 notes for under twenty shillings were prohibited by law in Scotland to prevent the circulation of worthless paper issued with no backing whatsoever.

The Scottish system differed from that of England in other ways too. Instead of one large bank of issue and a large number of small country issuers, Scotland at an early stage developed a system of regional banking, with many banks setting out to establish branches, so that to some degree, they prefigured the handful of clearing banks in modern Britain. Initially, banking in Scotland was very much a free-for-all. The two public banks might stand in lonesome grandeur, but the Scottish banks were not restricted as to the number of partners, so no institution was so powerful that it could control the others or serve as a lender of last resort. (Indeed, in 1793, the Scots found themselves having to go, cap in hand, to London to seek help from the Bank of England. It was not a relationship that they particularly enjoyed.) However, during the nineteenth century the long practice of the joint-stock approach resulted in a small group of large banks, who worked together effectively to create a coherent banking system.

When the Americans came to set up the Bank of North America in 1781, they had no local precedents to guide them. Indeed, given the shortage of hard money throughout the newly independent states, it is a matter of surprise that the Bank ever succeeded. Had it not been for the providential arrival of a shipment of French bullion in Philadelphia at a time when Robert Morris, the Superintendent of Finance and chief protagonist of the institution, could deposit some of this money in its vaults, it could never have commenced operations. This money soon had to be withdrawn, however, and the Bank, the only one chartered by both the Continental Congress, which represented all the colonies, and later by the state of Pennsylvania, was never able to avail itself of the opportunities opened to it by its charters.

Imitation is said to be the sincerest form of flattery, and Alexander Hamilton, Secretary of the Treasury, shamelessly flattered the British both in his funding programme and in his advocacy of a federally chartered bank. His funding programme created a mass of perpetual 3% consols in the British manner, but the idea never caught on. Americans of that era viewed a national debt as a national disgrace and the supposedly permanent 3% debt was quietly redeemed in the 1820s.

So far as the First Bank of the United States (1791–1811) was concerned, not only did Hamilton copy William Paterson's arguments in favour of the Bank of England, but many key provisions in the charter copied British precedents. Hamilton's Bank of the United States was clearly intended to be a miniature Bank of England.

The Americans copied the British, or used British precedents modified to local needs, in seven key banking areas. First there was debate over the use of government bonds as the basis of banking; second, there was disagreement as to whether the government and the bank should have a close relationship with regard to deposits, grants of monopoly and government members on the board of directors; third, there was a fierce battle over the denominations of notes to be issued by the bank; fourth, there was a savage struggle over whether the government should issue its own currency in lieu of that of a bank; fifth, there was a long-standing struggle over unit banking versus branch banking; sixth, there was a controversy over whether banking was a business to be open to anyone, or whether its practice should be limited to just a few institutions; finally, there were questions as to whether there should be a central bank to serve as a lender of last resort and, by extension, an argument as to what constituted a sufficient reserve, and what impact that reserve would have on the development of the economy. We shall examine these seven areas in turn.

As might be inferred from the facts given, the Bank of England began slowly because all its capital was tied up in government securities. The First Bank of the United States, aside from a promissory note given by the government for its 20% interest, had a capital consisting of $7,200,000 of Hamilton's new government bonds and only $800,000 in coin. The Second Bank (1816–36) had a coin-holding of only $2 million when it was supposed to have $7 million. Whether it could have raised that amount without disrupting the economy is questionable.

Now the Second Bank made itself unpopular with many parties. From 1817 to 1819 it encouraged a speculative boom but then sharply curtailed its loans, bringing on a depression. The public was further astonished when three men, a director of the parent bank together with the president and cashier of the Baltimore branch, were caught conspiring to obtain control of the bank by borrowing bank funds to buy stock without the pledge of collateral or permission for such loans from the branch or parent boards. This cost the bank nearly $1.8 million of its $35 million capital.

The public's tolerance for central banking was terminated by 'The Bank War', the political defects of Nicholas Biddle, third president of the Second Bank, and the bankruptcy of his bank. Thus, when the National Banks were set up in 1863, their contacts with the Federal Government were largely limited to the Comptroller of the Currency and his uniform currency. Similarly, when the Federal Reserve system was set up in 1913 with not one, but twelve banks of issue, the Central Board of Washington exercised only limited control over them. Not until Roosevelt's economic reforms in the New Deal of the 1930s did the Federal Reserve Board make the system act as a central bank.

The next question was whether to follow the policy of the Bank of England regarding the issue of notes under £5 ($25) which was backed by Adam Smith's advice on the point, or to copy the Scottish policy of lower denominations. Those who approved of the original practice of the Bank of France, which had a minimum 500 franc ($100) note, claimed that such a policy forced the acquisition and use of coins and the accumulation of bullion. The soundness of the Bank of England was cited in support of this contention, but the proponents of rapid speculative development and the Scottish system won. Coin was needed for foreign payments and America, in their view, simply did not have much hope of acquiring a large supply of bullion by trade to serve all the needs of commerce. State legislatures not only lowered the minimum note denomination to $5 (equal to the £1 Scottish notes) but backed even smaller bills. North Carolina, for example, had a $3 minimum, hence the survival of many $3 and $4 notes today. Other states allowed the issue of notes down to $1 and also fractional currency (parts of a dollar) in times of distress. These practices reflected the view that a predominantly metallic currency was unnecessarily costly and would impede the development of the country. Nor was any control exercised over design. As in the last sentence of the Book of Judges, 'every man did what was right in his own eyes'.

Next, there was a growing controversy as to whether the United States should not substitute a government for a bank currency. From the modern viewpoint, in an era of non-redeemable currencies, there is little to choose from, particularly with the bank's issues pretty much under the control of the Treasury. But in that era there were important differences. It should be remembered that it had originally been proposed that the Bank of England should merely circulate the government's notes. The Americans from 1690 onwards had issued colonial treasury notes and many looked back on that time with approval. The Constitution was silent on this point. Madison had proposed a clause to authorise such issues, but it had been voted down. So too, somewhat inconsistently, was an absolute ban on a government currency. The writers of the Constitution had clearly intended that the issue of a federal currency was not be lightly undertaken but the Treasury, during the War of 1812, had in desperation tried such issues and some people wanted more.

By the 1830s Jefferson, Madison, Jackson and a score of respected politicians and economists had backed the idea of a government currency. So, during the depression of 1837–43, did men like John C. Calhoun. In 1841 President Tyler came up with the idea of an Exchequer Bank with branches circulating and redeeming government notes and limited solely to being the government's banker. The idea was too novel for its time and eventually failed, but it foreshadowed many of the features of the Federal Reserve system.

Given this trend toward the use of a government currency, it is not surprising that both the United States and the Confederate States adopted a government currency system to finance their war efforts. Ironically, it was the Union which put into execution a nearer approximation of the system proposed by Calhoun than did the South, and was, in consequence, more successful in its policies. It is also interesting to note that when the Confederates had to choose a redemption clause for their notes, they copied verbatim the Bank of England's 'Six months after the ratification of peace . . .' clause when it suspended coin payments in 1797. The Southerners failed to remember the obvious point that the Bank of England had been unable to resume payments until 1821 – neither would the Confederacy have been able to honour its commitments had it survived.

The fifth point centred around the question of whether there was to be unit, as opposed to branch, banking. The first pointed to the English model in which the Bank of England was prominent, even when provincial banks set up branches, the second to Scottish methods, focusing rather on co-operation between several large joint-stock banks with branch networks.

Now, the part of the United States with the largest proportion of Scots or Scots-Irish settlers was in the slave-holding South. The First and Second Banks of the United States had both had numerous branches established long before the Bank of England set up its branches. Banks in Virginia, North and South Carolina, Georgia, Alabama and Mississippi (the last two before 1841) were all marked by branch banking. So, too, were Vermont (before 1812) and states such as Ohio and Indiana. Many of these banks also copied the Bank of England by keeping the same designs for their notes over a thirty-year period. But while England went over to the Scottish branch banking system after the Acts of 1826 and 1844, a process which gathered momentum with the emergence of the clearing banks in the early twentieth century, the Americans abandoned statewide branching systems in the 1860s, and only in the last twenty years have statewide and now interstate banks once more come into fashion. Before the 1860s such banks were thought to assure stability and safety by massing large capitals to assure the discharge of their debts. For the next hundred years unit banks were favoured, being apparently more responsive to public opinion.

As noted earlier, there was a heated debate over whether banking was a special business to be limited to the few or one that should, provided certain requirements could be met, be open to everyone. For the first generation after the Constitution was adopted, banks were set up by legislative enactment only, but by the 1830s this system, with its corruption, aspects of monopoly and the like, disappeared in favour of general incorporation laws.

However, the banks produced under these laws proved to be of very mixed quality. In Michigan, commissioners were circulated about the countryside to make sure that the banks were adhering to the terms of their charters as regards coin reserves and other matters. Also put into circulation were the pooled reserves of the banks, arriving at the next bank to be inspected just before the approach of the commissioners. Unfortunately for the banks, the commissioners altered their itinerary after one of them noted the similar composition of the coin reserves of each of the banks visited, and paid a surprise visit to a bank whose reserves proved to consist of a barrel of nails, with only the thinnest icing of gold coins at the top. 'The woods', the chief commissioner wrote in the report he sent to the legislature, 'were filled with the clink of fairy gold, but like the wind, none knew from whence it came or whither it was going.'

The last area of debate – the question of whether a central bank had any duty to shore up troubled banks and what sort of reserves were appropriate to perform that duty – was not something arrived at early in this story. Indeed, it does not seem to have become general policy until the 1820s in both the United States and Britain. The First Bank of the United States did not have to face any crashes or major bank runs and its only extant report, which survived Admiral Cockburn's and General Ross's arsonist visit to Washington in 1814, shows an institution carrying a 60% coin reserve against its liabilities, a ratio that made it almost bomb-proof. On the other hand, the Second Bank held only a 20% reserve that proved to be far too small even to protect itself. Moreover, unlike the Bank of England with its flexible rediscount rate, the Bank of the United States and American banks generally were prohibited by the usury laws from charging more than 6%. This meant either that the banks let people keep on borrowing far too long, or else they had summarily to slam shut the discount window on their customers' fingers.

Congress tried to correct this situation somewhat by forcing the National Banks to stay away from illiquid investments, and fixed cash reserves for banks in central reserve cities (25%) down to the reserves of country banks (10%). Here the trouble was that deposits with other National Banks counted as reserves, so that too many banks lent money at interest to the central reserve city banks. Naturally, at the very first hint of trouble the country banks recalled their deposits, forcing the major city banks to curtail their loans on a basis that fuelled, rather than stopped, panics. The crisis of 1907 provides a good example of this, clearly forcing the institution of the Federal Reserve system.

The Bank of England also faced such problems, but as a lender of last reserve it had a lender of last resort. Sir Arthur Conan Doyle's Sherlock Holmes tale, *The Red Headed League*, neatly illustrates the point, when the famous detective thwarted gangsters intent on looting the vault of a bank that had strengthened its reserves with French gold. On several occasions indeed, the Bank of France's gold was more than merely useful in heading off a suspension of the 1844 Bank Charter Act.

If a system of notes convertible into coin was to maintain itself, however, the reserve had to be kept high and this in turn meant that domestic budgets and trade balance sheets had to be kept in the black and that government intervention in the economy had to be limited without regard to domestic political considerations. Modern politicians, of course, do not like such discipline. Back in the 1960s, Dr John Kenneth Galbraith was summoned to Washington for the purpose of convincing the conservatives in the Senate that the gold cover should be removed from the Federal Reserve Notes. Appearing before Senator Harry F. Byrd Sr. of Virginia, who had misgivings on the subject, Galbraith quickly realised he had a problem on his hands. Trying to win the senator over, he pointed out that the gold cover was really unnecessary. Why, he noted, the Confederacy had fought a four-year war with less than $20 million in coin. 'Yes', said the Senator, 'but I think we all know what happened to the Confederacy.'

As far as note design is concerned, from 1791 to 1811 the First Bank of the United States and the Bank of England both produced notes of comparable technical quality. They had a small vignette, security paper and engraved lettering. Even while printing techniques became more sophisticated, such similarities persisted, but in the twentieth century, banknote designs have everywhere followed more nationalistic lines. One can hardly now mistake a German, French or British banknote for each other or for an American bill.

One reason why the Bank of England kept its designs simple and unchanging may have been because a master currency cannot frequently change its appearance without giving an impression of instability. Similarly, the United States currency has not changed much since 1928. Such changes as have occurred have involved a decline in technical execution, powered by the necessity of feeding an inflation that has seen the amount of currency outstanding rise by over ten times since 1969. Sad as it may be to those devoted to the art of the banknote, the American government is one of the most persistent advocates of the cashless society. Security justifications will no doubt provide a plausible pretext, but the government's desire to cut off tax evasion will be the real factor. As Murray T. Bloom noted long ago, governments are the ultimate counterfeiters.

In summation, there were many points on which the two English-speaking nations were paying attention to one another; there were others where each did what they wished and there were still others where they could agree to disagree. But regardless of what they did or how they did it, they had common goals and common problems, and they seldom, in their love-hate relationship, ignored one another.

Bibliography

CAMERON, ALAN, *Bank of Scotland 1695–1995. A Very Singular Institution*, Edinburgh and London 1995.

CHECKLAND, S.G., *Scottish Banking, A History 1695–1973*, Glasgow and London 1975.

CLAPHAM, SIR JOHN, *The Bank of England*, 2 vols., Cambridge 1944.

COTTRELL, P.L. AND ANDERSON, B.L. *Money and Banking in England: The Development of the Banking System 1694–1914*, London 1974.

HAMMOND, BRAY, *Banks and Politics in America from the Revolution to the Civil War*, Princeton 1967 (2nd edn 1991).

HURST, JAMES WILLARD, *A Legal History of Money in the United States, 1774–1970*, Nebraska 1973.

LEWIS, LAWRENCE, JR, *A History of the Bank of North America, the First Bank Chartered in the United States*, Philadelphia 1882.

NEWMAN, ERIC P., *The Early Paper Money of America*, 3rd edn, Iola, Wisconsin 1990.

PRESSNELL, L.S., *Country Banking in the Industrial Revolution*, Oxford 1956.

SAYERS, R.S., *The Bank of England 1891–1944*, Cambridge 1976.

SMITH, ADAM, *An Inquiry into the Nature and Causes of The Wealth of Nations*, 1776.

3

Paper for silver: Dutch coin notes and silver notes

H.W. Jacobi

The Kingdom of the Netherlands

After the collapse of Napoleon's Empire in 1814 the former Austrian Netherlands and the Dutch Republic were joined together to form the Kingdom of the Netherlands. The coins in circulation in the New Kingdom were the old coins from the Republic and the Austrian Netherlands; many French coins were also used in the south. The new government decided to choose the guilder (also known as 'gulden' and 'florin'), now divided into 100 cents, as the standard coin. The Coin Law of 1816 provided gold coins of ƒ10 and ƒ5, silver coins of ƒ3, ƒ1, ƒ½, 25 cents, 10 cents and 5 cents, and copper coins of 1 and ½ cent. The gold coins with the portrait of King William I were produced in large quantities, but only a small number of the silver coins were minted, because the silver content of the coins was a little too high compared with the gold, which forbade profitable minting.

De Nederlandsche Bank, or Dutch National Bank, was founded by Royal Decree of 25 March 1814. The Bank was granted a charter for twenty-five years and was allowed to issue banknotes in denominations from ƒ1,000 to ƒ25. The charter was renewed for another twenty-five years in 1838, and further extended in 1863 when it was also formally stated that the Bank should not issue notes below the value of ƒ25. Possibly because of negative memories of the French assignats of 1795, the Bank's notes were not very popular in the first half of the century and their circulation was limited. Furthermore, because of their high value the banknotes did not play an important part in the lives of most people: the lowest value of ƒ25 equalled the monthly wages of a workman!

The great recoinage

In 1830 the southern part of the Netherlands revolted and formed a separate state, the Kingdom of Belgium. Their standard coin was to be the Belgian franc, equal to the French franc. The now much smaller Northern Netherlands kept the rather grand name *Koninkrijk der Nederlanden*, that is, the Kingdom of the Netherlands. By a law of 1839 the silver content of the guilder was lowered and the ƒ3 coin was discontinued in favour of a coin of ƒ2.50. In 1847 a Coin Law was passed empowering the government to recoin the old silver coins of the Republic into a beautiful series of silver coins with a portrait of King William II. However, to make the recoinage possible great quantities of silver coin had to be temporarily taken out of circulation. To provide currency in the meantime, the government created paper money known as *muntbiljetten*, or coin notes.

The recoinage was regulated by a series of laws from 1845 to 1848. The lowest value allowed for the coin notes was ƒ1 and they were only to be issued against the full value of the silver taken in. The coin notes were thus fully backed and were to be seen as legal tender and used as cash money. The issue consisted of notes for ƒ500 (yellow), ƒ100 (blue) (fig. 1), ƒ20 (green), ƒ10 (purple) and ƒ5 (red). A design for a note of ƒ2.50 (black) was also produced, but it was never issued. As with the notes issued by the National Bank, the coin notes were printed by the Dutch security printer Johan Enschede en Zonen, in Haarlem. A total of ƒ30 million in coin notes was issued to cover the recoinage of a total of ƒ84 million of old silver coins. By the middle of 1847 there were enough new silver coins in circulation for the government to begin a gradual recall of the coin notes, the last of which was withdrawn on 31 December 1848.

After the successful recoinage of the Republican silver it was also possible to recall the silver and gold coins of the period after 1814. On 23 June 1850 the gold coins of ƒ10 and ƒ5 lost their status as legal tender. From that date on they could only be used as *negotiepenning*, that is, as trade coins without nominal value. Because the government foresaw that it would be impossible to exchange all gold coins for silver, a new series of coin notes was issued with four denominations: ƒ1,000 (green), ƒ500 (brown), ƒ100 (red) and ƒ10 (blue). The coin notes were to be backed by gold coins deposited at the National Bank and the law stated that all the coin notes should be recalled before 31 December 1852. ƒ30 million of coin notes were thought to be enough because most of the gold coins were outside the country, where they functioned as trade coins. From the total of ƒ172.5 million of gold coins struck, only about ƒ50 million were returned. Selling the gold at falling prices resulted in a net loss of ƒ1.2 million for the government. With this operation the great recoinage was completed. From 1 June 1851 the coin notes could be exchanged for silver, but the public liked using the notes, especially the ƒ10 note, and were very slow to convert them. Eventually the government was forced to extend their validity until 31 December 1853, and only by issuing new coin notes in 1852 was it possible to take the coin notes of 1849 out of circulation.

The financing of public debt with coin notes

A law of 1852 permitted the issue of coin notes for ƒ10, ƒ50 and ƒ100, the total value of which was to be limited to ƒ10 million. The money gained from this whole issue would be used to buy state obligations with an interest of 2.5 to 3% on the stock market. Because no interest had to be paid on coin notes, the government could save a little on its debt.

At first, from 1853 onwards, the government only issued coin notes of *f*10 (fig. 2). These finely engraved notes were very popular with the public as they formed a good intermediary between the highest coin with a value of *f*2.50 and the lowest banknote valued at *f*25. Moreover, at a time without instant money transfer by giro, the coin note of *f*10 was widely used for sending money by post. In 1878 a new type of coin note of *f*10 was issued; by virtue of its very elaborate printing it was better protected against forgery than the notes of the 1852 issue, which were by then very old-fashioned (fig. 3).

In 1884 the total value of the coin notes in circulation was raised to *f*15 million and, at the same time, coin notes for a value of *f*50 were created, with yet another design. This blue note, issued between 1885 and 1897, carries a small medallion in the right-hand border with a portrait of King William III. The same design was also used for the brown coin notes of *f*10 issued from 1894 to 1898, with a portrait of Wilhelmina as a child (fig. 4), and then from 1900 to 1903 with a portrait showing her as newly crowned queen.

The coin notes were nearing their end, however. More and more politicians thought them to be undesirable, and on their initiative the government passed the laws of 1903 and 1904 which ended the circulation of coin notes. All coin notes issued under the laws of 1852 and 1884 were withdrawn by 1 April 1904. The National Bank took over the public debt of *f*15 million and, to replace the popular coin note of *f*10, the Bank was now allowed to issue its own note for *f*10. At the same time the bank-notes were given legal tender status, which had been denied them until that time. With this action the circulation of the coin notes was brought to an end, fifty-eight years after their creation.

The First World War

This perfect situation could not last. With the outbreak of the First World War in August 1914, people in the Netherlands were uncertain about the likelihood of the country being able to maintain its neutral position. In July 1914 the public had already started to take their savings out of the post offices and banks and to change them into silver. And, because the public kept the silver coins in their pockets, there was from the beginning of August a great shortage of silver coins in circulation. To facilitate the payment of wages and social security benefits many municipalities and companies were forced to issue their own emergency notes. The government reacted quickly. On the night of 3 August they decided in consultation with the director of the National Bank to create a 'paper auxiliary money', and on 6 August 1914 a new law was passed, allowing the issue of *zilverbons*, or silver notes, this new name almost certainly being used so that the government would not be seen to reintroduce coin notes only ten years after their abolition. The new silver notes consisted of a *f*1 note (brown), a *f*2.50 note (blue-green) and a *f*5 note (green) (fig. 5). Because of the great hurry the notes were to be printed by an Amsterdam security printer, De Bussy. They were of a rather simple design and printed on one side only. Furthermore, they did not have individual serial numbers, but only a series number; ten thousand notes in each series were printed. On 7 August the first notes were delivered to the National Bank. When they were put into circulation, however, there turned out to be little demand for a note of ƒ5, so only the relatively small number of 547,200 such notes were issued.

The simple uniface design of the silver note of 1914 was easily forged, and although the number of forgeries was small, the government decided to issue a new series of silver notes. These notes were also printed on only one side, but they had watermarked paper and individual serial numbers. This second series of silver notes consisted of notes of ƒ1 (brown) and ƒ2.50 (blue), with issue dates in 1915, 1916 and 1917. However, to their dismay the government found that these new silver notes, especially the ƒ2.50, were counterfeited very fast and in great numbers!

Such a problem demanded a radical solution, and another new design was produced, now printed on both sides with a border of complicated guilloches. As an extra precaution against forgery paper with coloured threads was used. First a note of ƒ2.50 was issued with dates of 1918 to 1922. This was followed by a ƒ1 note with an issue date of 1920 only. Against all expectation it was discovered after a few years that there were again good forgeries on the market. The paper of the forgeries lacked the coloured threads, but because of the very detailed printing this was not obvious. So in 1922 the design was changed and the middle of the reverse was left almost bare so that the coloured threads could easily be seen. The government planned to replace the silver notes with silver coins of ƒ1 and ƒ2.50, but this ambition was frustrated by high silver prices after the war. Just as in 1839, it was only possible to strike new coins after a debasement, now from 0.945 to 0.700 silver. The new coins had a fourth portrait of Queen Wilhelmina; the ƒ1 coins were struck from 1922 onwards, and the ƒ2.50 coins from 1929 onwards. When enough coins had been put into circulation the silver notes were withdrawn and stored at the National Bank.

The Second World War

On 10 May 1940 German soldiers invaded the Netherlands and after five days of hard battle and bombardment of Rotterdam the Dutch surrendered. Queen Wilhelmina and the government had to escape to England. From the outbreak of the war the public had started hoarding their silver coins, a small security in a very insecure world. Faced by growing shortages of silver coin, the National Bank was again forced to put silver notes into circulation. From 20 May 1940 onwards silver notes of ƒ1 and ƒ2.50 were issued, consisting not only of the old notes that had been lying in the vaults of the Bank, but also of new notes that the government had had made when the threat of war was felt in 1938. Just as in 1914, many municipalities were forced to issue local emergency notes in the first week after the outbreak of war. However, as soon as the silver notes arrived in the municipal treasuries, the production of local notes was stopped, sometimes even before they were put into circulation.

The designs of the silver notes of October 1938 were based on those of the issue of 1918–27, but now the centre of both the front and back was unprinted so that the coloured threads of the paper were clearly visible (fig. 6). The silver note of ƒ1 (brown) bore a great resemblance to the earlier issue, but the note of ƒ2.50 was rather different, especially on the reverse. With the continuing demand for notes with low values, like the banknotes of ƒ10 and ƒ20, it was decided in the last year of the war to issue a silver note for ƒ5 (green). The scarcity of resources in the last months of 1944 resulted in a relatively simple note on plain paper.

In 1942 the Dutch government in exile in London began preparations for circulating currency in the Netherlands after the war. In the winter of 1942–3 secret discussions were held on an emergency financial policy. On the advice of the Minister of Finance, the government decided to issue *biljetten aan toonder*, that is, treasury notes payable on demand. The Minister was given permission to issue notes in denominations of ƒ0.50 and higher, with a maximum value of ƒ100 million. Article 5 of the Royal Decree shows that the government intended to exchange the paper money already in circulation in the Netherlands for these new notes, which were to be printed by the American Bank Note Company in New York. In April 1944 the government also placed an order for the production of silver coins of 10 and 25 cents in the United States, which resulted in the notes for ƒ0.50 being deemed unnecessary. Later that year the total value of the notes was raised to ƒ300 million.

On the notes printed by the American Bank Note Company we meet again the familiar name of *muntbiljet*, or coin note (fig. 7). It is not known why this old name was adopted again, but it is safe to assume that the government wanted to make a clear distinction between the new notes and the banknotes and silver notes that had been in circulation during the occupation of the Netherlands, and therefore fell back on the nineteenth-century name. In spring 1944 the first chests containing the coin notes arrived in London, and in the autumn of 1944 they were given to the advancing Allied troops. After the liberation of Maastricht, the first city to be liberated in the Netherlands, on 13 and 14 September *Het Militair Gezag*, the Military Powers, started using the coin notes. It was feared that the amount printed would be insufficient, and an order for another ƒ300 million was given to the American Bank Note Company.

Black marketeers and money speculators in the Netherlands were immediately interested in the new coin notes, thinking that they would be excluded from any imminent monetary reform. As a result, in December 1944 the Chief of Staff of the Military Forces was forced to decree that the Dutch government would not at that time or in the future discriminate between the new coin notes and the notes that were issued before or during the war.

After the Second World War

The liberation of the Netherlands took until May 1945, by which time the coin notes of 1943 were thoroughly mixed in with the circulating banknotes and silver notes and therefore could not be excluded from monetary reform. Thus it was again necessary for the government to order new paper money. For the sake of speed it was decided to have the notes printed in England. The government ordered coin notes of ƒ1 and ƒ2.50 and Bank issues of ƒ10, ƒ20, ƒ25, ƒ50, ƒ100 and ƒ1,000 notes, all with the date 7 May

1945. Several different printing firms were used: the coin notes and the banknotes of *f*10 and *f*20 were printed by Thomas De La Rue in London and the banknote of *f*1,000 by Waterlow & Sons, also in London, while Johan Enschede en Zonen in Haarlem, the usual printer of Dutch banknotes, printed notes of *f*10, *f*25, *f*50 and *f*100.

The monetary reform, for which the Belgian reform served as an example, is firmly linked with the name of the then Minister of Finance, Lieftinck, under whose direction this gigantic operation was executed. On 16 September 1945 all paper money lost the status of legal tender and all bank and giro accounts were stopped. Every Dutchman received 10 guilders for one week's cost of living, the so-called *'tientje van Lieftinck'*, or 'ten guilders of Lieftinck'. Much money, black-market profits, lost its value, because the owners could not prove that it came from legal sources. However, as churches were free of any obligation to reveal the source of their money, they received many large donations and so the ill-gotten gains served a good purpose in the end.

The ten guilders of Lieftinck consisted of new coin notes printed in England with the date 18 May 1945; two *f*2.50 and five *f*1 notes. To distinguish the new notes from the series of 1943 the profile of the queen looked the other way, to the right. Just what *f*10 per person meant is clearly illustrated by the story of an inhabitant of the town of Harderwijk. This man, the owner of a small bakery, had a wife and twelve children. For this family, therefore, he received fourteen times *f*10, a total of *f*140. With that money this small shopkeeper was for a week the richest man in town! At the beginning of October the banknotes printed in Haarlem came into circulation, and step by step in the following years the restrictions of monetary reform were lifted.

On 1 September 1948 Queen Wilhelmina abdicated in favour of her daughter, Juliana, and the new queen's portrait was placed on coins and notes. New coin notes for *f*1 (brown) and *f*2.50 (blue) with the date 8 August 1949 were again printed by Johan Enschede en Zonen in Haarlem. The country was still too poor after the war to afford the luxury of silver coins, so by the Bank Law of 1948 the smallest denomination for banknotes was lowered from *f*10 to *f*5 in order to facilitate the abolition of coin notes in the future.

Only by the beginning of the 1950s was the Dutch economy so far restored that it was possible to think about issuing silver coins of *f*1 and *f*2.50. New silver guilders, starting with the date of 1954, were issued from 1956 onwards. When in 1958 there were enough coins in circulation, the government started to withdraw the coin notes of one guilder. In 1961 the silver coins of *f*2.50 with dates of 1959 onwards were put into circulation and the use of coin notes rapidly diminished. The silver coins were in use for only a short period, however, for silver speculation in 1967 resulted in that metal becoming so expensive that the intrinsic value of the coins surpassed their nominal value. From then on they were made of nickel. The issue of the coin notes for *f*2.50 ceased in 1967, though they remained in circulation for a number of years. They disappeared only gradually as they were withdrawn from circulation by the National Bank and it was not until 1987 that the last coin note lost its status as legal tender.

From this date onwards the Dutch circulation has been as it should be: for the lower denominations coins are used, produced by the Dutch Mint on behalf of the government, and for the higher values there are banknotes, still printed by Johan Enschede and Sons and issued by the Dutch National Bank. Because the present-day coins no longer contain precious metal, there is no need to fear hoarding in times of insecurity, and so the role of coin notes and silver notes in Dutch monetary history has finally come to an end.

Glossary
of Dutch paper money terms

Bankbiljet Banknote, paper money issued by *De Nederlandsche Bank*, the Dutch National Bank, by virtue of a government charter. Banknotes are meant to provide permanent currency for higher amounts.

Betaalt aan Toonder Pays on demand.

Koninklijk Besluit (KB) Royal Decree.

Muntbiljet Treasury Note (literally: coin note), temporary paper currency issued by *De Minister van Financiën*, the Treasury Department, in situations where a shortage of coins in circulation occurs or is foreseen. There is no fundamental difference between coin notes and silver notes other than the name.

Muntwet Coin Law.

Staatscourant (Stcrt.) State publication, daily information paper of the government.

Staatsblad (Stb). State publication, official publication of all laws and Royal Decrees of the Netherlands.

Wet Law.

Wettig betaalmiddel Legal tender.

zilverbon Treasury Note (literally: silver note), temporary paper currency issued by *De Minister van Financiën*, the Treasury Department, in situations where a shortage of coins in circulation occurs or is foreseen. There is no fundamental difference between coin notes and silver notes other than the name.

Bibliography

ERP, ROB VAN, *Vergeefsche jacht op 'valsche zilverbons'*, Amsterdam 1988.

GROLLE, JAN J., *Geschiedenis van het Nederlandse Bankbiljet*, Bussum 1991.

JACOBI, HANS, AND BEEK, BERT VAN, *Geld van het Koninkrijk Amsterdam 1988*.

MEVIUS, J. AND LELIVELT, F.G., *Speciale catalogus van de Nederlandse bankbiljetten van 1814 tot heden*, 2nd edn, Vriezenveen 1981.

NIEBOER, WILLEM J., *Onze bevrijdingsbiljetten 1943–1945*, Groningen 1992.

PICK, ALBERT, *Standard Catalog of World Paper Money*, vol. 2, 7th edn, Iola, Wisconsin 1994.

PICK ALBERT, AND SIEMSEN, CARL, *Das Notgeld des II Weltkrieges*, Munich 1979.

Staatsblad van het Koninkrijk der Nederlanden, 1814-heden (Official State Publication of Laws and Royal Decrees of the Netherlands)

VERKOOYEN, J.M.H.F.M., *Catalogus van het Nederlands noodgeld van de eerste wereldoorlog en het interbellum*, Maastricht 1994.

VRIES, JOHAN DE, *Geschiedenis van de Nederlandsche Bank, 1914 tot 1948*, Amsterdam 1989.

1 Coin note for 100 guilders, 1 January 1846.

2 Coin note for 10 guilders, 1 September 1866.

3 (*left*) Coin note for 10 guilders, 29 September 1886.

4 (*left, below*) Coin note for 10 guilders, 15 January 1897.

5 (*right*) Silver note for 5 guilders, 7 August 1914.

6 (*right*) Silver note for 2.50 guilders, 1 October 1938.

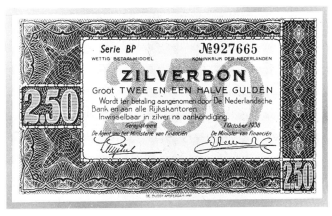

7 (*below*) Coin note for 100 guilders, 4 February 1943.

4

Louis Kossuth's banknote issue and legal case in London in 1861

Erika Garami

At the time of the Revolution and War of Independence of 1848–9 Louis Kossuth[1] became Minister of Finance of the first Hungarian independent government. He reorganised Hungarian financial affairs, and issued the first coins and banknotes with a Hungarian legend, replacing the previous Latin coin legends and German banknote legends. In Hungary no independent national bank existed at that time, as efforts to establish one had always been suppressed by the Habsburgs. In the whole Habsburg Empire the circulating paper money consisted only of the notes of the National Bank of Austria (founded in 1816); the same was true in Hungary, although the notes were never accepted legally by that country.

After the suppression of the War of Independence in 1849, Kossuth and other revolutionary leaders were forced to leave Hungary, but until the Compromise of 1867, which established the dual Austro-Hungarian monarchy, Kossuth continued to make preparations for a second war of independence (which was never realised), organising the army, and a new series of money. According to his plan the soldiers would have received his proposed notes as payment.

Kossuth was interned in Turkey, but managed to leave in 1851 with English and American help. First he spent three victorious weeks in England making a series of public speeches, then he sailed for the United States, where he issued dollar bonds in New York (fig. 1) and forint notes in Philadelphia. In July 1852 he returned to Europe, to live in London for nine years.[2] After a period of no numismatic importance when he was active as an English journalist,[3] Kossuth revived his activities as a political exile. In September 1860, after discussions with Count Cavour, Prime Minister of Piedmont, and Emperor Napoleon III, preparations were made for a series of Hungarian notes issued from London. Kossuth's priority was paper money, but he also wanted to strike base metal coins, in smaller quantities.[4] He hoped to have the coins struck in either Italy or Switzerland, but in fact the whole issue of coinage remained only a plan though it was rumoured that Kossuth hoped to raise one of Queen Victoria's sons to the Hungarian throne, and that coins were issued bearing his portrait.[5]

The first task was to issue banknotes. Originally Cavour offered 500,000 francs to the Hungarians, out of which 200,000 francs were aimed at the banknote issue. By mistake only half the money was remitted to the bankers, Hambro, in London, but the printers, who had already started production, were not willing to wait any longer, and it was vital to keep the printing secret. Cavour insisted on the notes being printed in London so that the help of the Turin government should not become known.[6] Later, Cavour lost interest in Hungarian affairs and would have preferred to stop printing the Hungarian notes,[7] but it was too late for that.

A former American consul, Rodney Croskey, acted as the middleman between Kossuth and Day & Son, the lithographic printing firm in England chosen to produce the notes. Day & Son had been founded by William Day senior in about 1823, and became known for its early use of chromolithography, which was later raised to a very high standard by the firm of Thomas De La Rue, one of the most outstanding banknote printers of the age. Both firms would have played an important part in Kossuth's plan if he had been able to send the notes to Hungary via Genoa as intended.[8]

Remembering the lack of small change during the Revolution, Kossuth planned to issue only small denomination notes, of one, two, and five forints. In late 1860 Day & Son was given an order for 21 million Hungarian notes at a price of £8,000. Such a quantity was too large to keep secret, for fifty printing machines were only able to produce one million notes a week,[9] so that additional machines and workers had to be taken on. The banknote paper bears a simplified version of the arms of Hungary with the legend 'RESURGO' in the watermark (fig. 2). Unfortunately, there is no primary source available, but the paper was probably produced by Samuel Leyh.[10] The forerunners of the London notes were the 1848 issue in Hungary (fig. 3), to which the London notes are similar in size, but simpler in design and with less ornamentation (figs 4,5,6). As these notes are one-sided, they do not carry the penal clause, which has been printed in five languages on the Hungarian issue. On the London notes only the denomination can be found in five languages. The text of the note in English is:

ONE FLORIN

THE MONETARY NOTE WILL BE RECEIVED IN EVERY HUNGARIAN STATE AND PUBLIC PAY OFFICE AS ONE FLORIN IN SILVER, THREE ZWANZIGGERS [twenties] BEING ONE FLORIN: AND ITS WHOLE NOMINAL VALUE IS GUARANTEED BY THE STATE.

LOUIS KOSSUTH
IN THE NAME OF THE NATION

The place and date of issue is not indicated. At the bottom the royal arms of Hungary can be seen and the notes carried printed serial numbers of five digits.[11]

Kossuth wanted to divide the twenty-three tons of notes into smaller portions and send them to Genoa. His plan was to store the notes safely there together with the coat of arms of Hungary, until the right moment came to send them to Hungary. Shipments were planned for the middle of February 1861. Kossuth made an agreement with an old friend, Charles Rawlins, a Liverpool merchant, to store the notes in Lancashire for three months. However, when most of the notes had already been prepared a 1 forint note somehow came into the hands of an English policeman, an occurrence which led eventually to the case in Chancery between Kossuth and Emperor Franz Joseph. Sir Richard Mayne, Chief Commissioner of the Metropolitan Police, when informed of the note, required the printers to 'detain all the Hungarian notes'.[12] How did the English police become possessed of the note and by what authority did the Chief Commissioner require Day & Son to suspend the manufacture of the notes? Such questions were raised in the House of Commons at the time and are still of interest today.

Before Kossuth started issuing Hungarian banknotes in England, he had asked for legal advice. Prominent lawyers such as George Denman, Thomas Welsby and Joshua Toulmin Smith advised that only imitating current notes was illegal by British law. As early as 6 February 1861 the Home Office already possessed the seized 1 forint note, which was shown as an exhibit at the hearings. The Foreign Secretary advised the Home Secretary to order the Chief Commissioner to obtain examples of the Kossuth notes 'by amicable transaction' and to arrange the matter quietly.[13]

It seems likely that an Austrian agent must have been among the workers who had been additionally taken on by Day & Son in order to speed up printing. Emperor Franz Joseph was concerned about the activities of Hungarian revolutionary refugees and after having made unsuccessful attempts to prevent the manufacture of the Kossuth notes, first through diplomatic channels, then through criminal procedure, he entered a claim to Chancery by the Austrian ambassador, Count Rudolph Apponyi, expecting Kossuth to withdraw from the legal case because of the high costs.

The case for the plaintiff was undertaken by Freshfields & Newman (still existing as Freshfields today), who had long been acting also as solicitors and attorneys to the Bank of England. Curiously the Lord Chancellor, Roundell Palmer (later Earl of Selbourne), had himself started his career in 1839 as a lawyer in Freshfields & Newman – it was his final decision which put an end to the Kossuth case. Ashurst & Morris (Ashurst Morris Crisp today) undertook the defence of Kossuth, despite strong opposition from Toulmin Smith, who said, 'It is the greatest misfortune that the case got into Ashurst's hands . . . no doubt he felt a sincere wish to help: but he is not the man for the job.'[14] Lake & Kendall acted for the printers.

The plaintiff, Franz Joseph, acting as King of Hungary (though he was not in fact crowned until 1867), sued to have the notes and plates delivered up and to restrain the manufacture of any further notes, claiming that the issue of such notes would injure his rights by promoting revolution. Furthermore, he claimed that he had never authorised Kossuth to use the royal arms of Hungary. Kossuth had to answer in eight days and raise the legal costs, not only for himself, but also for the printers, who would otherwise have withdrawn from the case.

The two Kossuth affidavits could not have been prepared without the professional help of Toulmin Smith. Several newspapers, including even *The Times*, which was pro-Austrian, published the full texts. They were also translated and published in several European newspapers. In his affidavits Kossuth denied that the plaintiff was King of Hungary, thus claiming that he had no right to suit as plaintiff before the English Court, and had no authority to issue notes without the previous consent of the Hungarian Diet (parliament). It was further stated that the only person to whom the Diet ever gave such permission in Hungary was Kossuth, in 1848 when he was

Minister of Finance and in 1849 as Governor of Hungary. Kossuth also argued that the arms of Hungary were not royal but national, and that any Hungarian might lawfully use them. It was as a national emblem that they were introduced into the notes. The royal prerogative in Hungary referred only to coins (gold and silver), not to banknotes. The notes printed by Day & Son could only be put into circulation under the consent of the Hungarian Diet.

At first Kossuth hoped for a favourable judgement, or at least a successful appeal,[15] but the Vice Chancellor found in favour of Franz Joseph, though the strength of Kossuth's affidavits was acknowledged by the Court. The appeal was heard before Lord Campbell, then Lord Chancellor. Instead of emphasising the royal prerogative and the prevention of revolution, the plaintiff now focused on injury to property. If Kossuth's London notes were introduced in Hungary, they would create a 'spurious circulation and detriment to the State', in the words of the Lord Chancellor.

Kossuth denied that he would circulate these notes as long as the present conditions existed. They would later replace the existing issue, which would depreciate during the revolution. Finally, the Lord Chancellor affirmed the Vice Chancellor's decree, with the modification that the arms might be used by all Hungarians. One of the judges, Lord Justice Knight Bruce, proposed that instead of the plaintiff, the defendants should pay for the costs. The notes and the plates should be delivered up to the plaintiff for destruction, and he should pay the value of the paper if it were sold for the purpose of being converted into pulp.[16]

Theoretically, Kossuth, who had already moved to Italy, could have appealed to the House of Lords, but he did not want to, partly because he was disappointed by the English jurisdiction, and partly because he did not have the necessary £3,000 or £4,000, especially after the death of his main supporter, Cavour, in June 1861. A jury consisting of Tory lawyers and the Lord Chancellor would hardly have decided in his favour. He was right: one of the judges, Hugh Cairns, wrote to the Austrian ambassador right after the case, 'An Appeal to the House of Lords would be hopeless'.[17] In order to cover the law costs, Kossuth obtained £1,000 from Napoleon III, and £2,000 from Cavour. The total sum due is not known, as he had to pay in smaller amounts (for example, stamp-duties, the solicitors' fees and so on). According to the statement of charges and disbursements by Ashurst & Morris,[18] the total was £1,365 7s 7d, but that does not include, for example, the costs of the hearings before the Chancellor.

Although the legal action prevented the production of the Hungarian notes, the matter had not been settled yet. There was almost another legal case over the price of the pulp, £336 18s, which was to be paid for by the plaintiff, but the question was, to whom? – to the printers, or to Kossuth, who had paid for the paper earlier? Finally, though, no case was brought over this, or over monies which had been promised to middlemen if the notes were successfully sent out of England.

Kossuth's London banknote case was not restricted to Chancery Lane: it caused debates in the House of Commons and in the newspapers, and pamphlets were written both for and against his case. The public seemed to give its support to Kossuth. *The Parliamentary Remembrancer*[19] published by Joshua Toulmin Smith contained not only the speeches and what had been said in the sessions of the House of Commons, but also commentaries on behalf of Kossuth. Toulmin Smith's name is linked also with the best pamphlet written on the case: *Who is the King of Hungary that is now suitor in the English Court of Chancery? A letter to Lord John Russell.*[20] Three thousand copies were sent to Members of Parliament and newspaper editors, and it was published in translation in France and Germany. Toulmin Smith wrote other works, too, in favour of the Hungarian exile.[21] Naturally, 'the other side' did not leave these publications unanswered.[22]

Kossuth always emphasised the importance of the press[23] and organised the activity of Hungarian political refugees all over Europe. In London, the *Daily News*, the *Morning Chronicle* and *The Economist* – among others – published their articles, and papers elsewhere in Britain, in Manchester, Liverpool and even Scotland, reported the case. In the end, only *The Times* remained on the Austrian side.

Interestingly enough, none reported on the cancellation of the notes. About twenty million pieces in sixty boxes were delivered on 22 July 1861 to Freshfields & Newman, solicitors to the Bank of England, who undertook to destroy them by fire in the presence of representatives of both parties.[24] Apparently, the burning lasted for two weeks in the ovens of the Bank of England, and cost the plaintiff £200.

A few specimens survived, having been exhibits at the hearings, or illegally stolen by workers in the printing works, or during the burning in the Bank. Some notes which escaped burning were lost or destroyed during the Second World War, but the most famous lost pieces sank on the *Titanic*. The number of pieces still existing is very low: four examples of 1 forint, eight of 2 forint and four of the 5 forint notes. Thus only sixteen pieces are known altogether, in either public or private collections.

With regard to the printers, Day & Son, a decline in their fortunes after prosperity in the 1850s was not helped by the Kossuth case, but it did not bring catastrophe either, for press and public opinion sympathised with them. At the final hearing before the Lord Chancellor the conclusion was: 'Our sympathy has been powerfully appealed to in favour of the Messrs Day . . . They, no doubt, would have derived much profit, as well as fame, if Hungary had been revolutionised by their means, they must console themselves with the reflection that they have failed in a great enterprise.'[25]

A stationer bought the three tons of paper with the 'RESURGO' watermark, made them into envelopes, and sold them. Many of them were sent by the Hungarian emigrés all over Europe. It is not known who this stationer was; he may have been the same person who bought the property near Kingsway in Holborn from the Days in 1861.

Interesting pieces of news appeared in the newspapers; for instance, in the *Edinburgh News and Literary Chronicle* on 22 June: 'Kossuth carried with him a portable press for printing those notes which the law does not permit him to obtain in this country.' The news turned out, of course, to be false. Some months after the case in Chancery a Glasgow glass and ceramics manufacturer, John MacAdam, tried to persuade Kossuth to appeal to the Scottish parliament, but all his efforts were in vain. An Italian sequel to Kossuth's London note issue took place five years later in 1866 in Turin. The new designs were entirely different from the London ones. However, due to the political changes no printing was possible, and the copper plates and some specimens of those notes can thus be regarded as the last signs of the note issue planned by the Hungarian exile after the 1848–9 Revolution.

Abbreviations

Irataim Kossuth, Lajos, *Irataim az emigrációból* (*Memories from My Exile*), vol. III, Budapest 1881
MEPO Metropolitan Police
MOL Magyar Országos Levéltár (Hungarian National Archive), Budapest
OSZK Kt Országos Széchényi Könyvtár, Kézirattár (Hungarian National Széchényi Library, Manuscripts), Budapest
PRO Public Record Office, London

Notes

1. Louis Kossuth (1802–94) was a lawyer and journalist who became a key figure in Hungary's struggle for independence from Austria. For some years after the suppression of the Revolution of 1848–9, he continued his campaign as a political exile in England, but spent his last years in loneliness in Italy. Despite his brief period of power, he remained a world-famous symbol of revolutionary nationalism.
2. Jánossy, Dénes, *A Kossuth-emigráció Angliaban es Amerikaban* (*The Kossuth Exile in England and in America*), *1851–52*, vols I–II, Budapest 1940, 1944, 1948. Balassa, József, *Kossuth Amerikában* (*Kossuth in America*), *1851–52*, Budapest 1931.
3. Haraszti, H. Éva, *Kossuth as an English Journalist*, Budapest 1990.
4. Kossuth writing to Ferenc Pulszky, London, 1 October 1860. MOL R 90 I 2904.
5. Berzeviczy, Albert, *Az abszolutizmus kora Magyarországon* (*The Age of Absolutism in Hungary*), *1848–65*, vol. I, Budapest 1922. The rumours were unfounded.
6. Ferenc Pulszky writing to Kossuth, Turin, 8 and 13 October. MOL R 90 I 3399 and 2891.
7. György Klapka writing to László Teleki, Naples, 18 November 1860, in Ács, Tivadar, *A genovai lázadás* (*Revolt in Genoa*), *1859–61*, Budapest 1958.
8. *Irataim* III, p. 368. Kossuth's plan was to print

the notes in London, store them in Liverpool, and then ship them to Hungary, via De La Rue's office in Genoa, and the governor of Ancona, who was pro-Hungarian.
9. *Irataim* III, pp. 74–5.
10. Ambrus, Béla, 'Kossuth Lajos londoni bankópere 1861–62' ('Louis Kossuth's London banknote case'), *Levéltár Szemle* 28 (1978), 3, p. 639.
11. Pick, Albert, *Standard Catalog of World Paper Money, vol. I, Specialised Issues*, 6th edn, Iola, Wisconsin, 1991, Hungary nos S146, 147, 148.
12. PRO MEPO 1 46.
13. PRO Russell Papers 30/22, 14B 155.
14. J. Toulmin Smith writing to Ferenc Pulszky, London, 14 March 1861. OSZK Kt Fond VIII/1080.
15. Kossuth writing to János Ludvigh, 15 April and Kossuth to Miklós Kiss, London, 17 April 1861. MOL R 90 I 3711 and 3714.
16. PRO C33/1077 MOL R 115. 3566.
17. Hugh Cairns to Count Rudolph Apponyi, London, 12 June 1861. OSZK Kt Fond II/94.
18. MOL R 115. 3319.
19. *The Parliamentary Remembrancer,* vol. IV, Session 1861. Conducted by Toulmin Smith of Lincoln's Inn, Office of the 'Parliamentary Remembrancer', London 1861.
20. By Toulmin Smith of Lincoln's Inn, London 1861.
21. For example, *Illustrations of the Political and Diplomatic Relations of the Independent Kingdom of Hungary and of the interest that Europe has in the 'Austrian Alliance'*, London 1861.
22. For example, *The Emperor of Austria versus Louis Kossuth. A few words of common sense, based on documentary evidence and historical facts*, by an Hungarian author of 'Civilisation in Hungary', London 1861.
23. Kossuth writing to János Ludvigh, London, 28 February 1861. MOL R 115. 3166.
24. PRO C31, 1544 2nd part.
25. *The Law Journal Reports from Michaelmas Term 1860 to Trinity Term 1861*, vol. XXXIX, new series XXX, part I, Chancery and Bankruptcy (MDCCCLXI), Edwrd Bret Ince, p. 708.

1   Hungarian Fund, $100, printed by Danforth, Bald & Co., New York, 1852.

2   RESURGO watermark of the London note.

3   Note for 5 forint, Buda-Pest, 1848 (obverse).

4 Note for 1 forint, printed by Day
& Son, London, 1861.

5 Note for 2 forint, printed by Day
& Son, London, 1861.

6 Note for 5 forint, printed by Day
& Son, London, 1861.

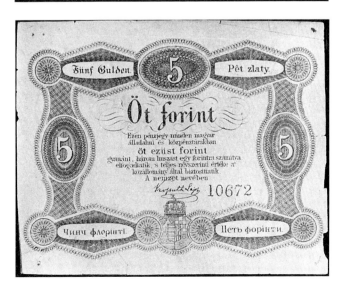

5

Economic warfare: banknote forgery as a deliberate weapon

Peter Bower

For as long as money has been made it has been counterfeited, usually by individuals or small groups of people motivated primarily by greed. But by far the largest and most successful counterfeiting projects have been conceived and executed for political motives rather than mere avarice. This paper will deal with two such forms of economic warfare. The first example is one directed by a government against an enemy: the British forgery of French assignats in the early 1790s. The second example is somewhat different: the thirty-five year career of a late nineteenth-century master forger and the group of people around him, whose main aim appears to have been the destabilisation of the currencies of Russia, France and Britain for political ends.[1]

The deliberate forgery by one government or power of another's currency is not new. As early as 1470, Duke Galeazzo Sforza of Milan counterfeited the money of Venice in an attempt to damage the respectability and reputation of Venetian bankers. Nor was the forgery of French assignats the first occasion that the British had resorted to such activities: they had already copied the currency of the infant United States during the War of Independence.

The use of forgery as hostile economic manipulation has continued right up to the present time. During the occupation of Vienna in 1806 Napoleon had copies made of the plates for notes issued by the Wiener-Stadt-Banco, and he later printed this Austrian currency in both Paris and Italy. Napoleon also had both 25 rouble and 50 rouble Russian State Credit Notes (assignats) counterfeited between 1805 and 1812 in an effort to destabilise a financial system already burdened by massive devaluation. There is some evidence that he also attempted the forgery of English banknotes during the same period.[2] During the Second World War the United States counterfeited Japanese currency, and the author John Steinbeck tried to persuade Franklin D. Roosevelt to flood Germany with notes from the air. The Germans themselves, in both Operation Andrew and Operation Bernhard, produced some of the best forgeries of British banknotes ever made.

Forgery for personal gain has always attracted its fair share of skilled but flawed individuals. An Austrian, Peter Ritter von Behr, embarked on a series of exceptionally high quality forgeries after the failure of his business ventures in 1839. When he and his wife were arrested in 1845 he admitted only to producing as much as they had needed at any one time and denied that his wife knew anything of his activities. In Britain in the 1960s and 1970s Charles Black produced quite high quality forged notes, but again he was caught and spent some years in gaol. However, Leon Warnerke, the individual whose story I shall tell in the second part of this paper, is of a different calibre altogether. In thirty-five years of activity, producing Russian, French and English notes between c. 1865 and 1900, he was never caught, although he came very close. Indeed it is only in the past three years that his activities have come to light with the discovery of a hoard of his trials, notes, letters and documents, and equipment. Politics played a great part in his operation, at least initially, and remained an important motive for many of his co-conspirators throughout, although it has become obvious as I have researched this particular project that the sheer challenge of the job, the intricate workmanship involving complex printing skills, chemistry, watermarking and paper-making knowledge, probably acted increasingly as Warnerke's motivation.

What both the British forgery of assignats and Warnerke's operation have in common, besides the attempt to wreck or at least destabilise a government's economy, is that in both cases the different skills and techniques involved were at their time right at the forefront of developments in various technologies. The manufacture of genuine assignats had involved great and very effective experimentation in a number of disciplines – in the development of security and chiaroscuro watermarking, changes in paper technology (in the bleaching and beating of rags for example), in the mechanics of printing (the rapid development of stereotype and polytype techniques), in engraving methods and in the hardening of metal plates and punches. The forgery of these notes involved an equal expertise as well as considerable time, trouble and expense, and led to equivalent developments in Britain in the technical areas outlined above. Warnerke's use and development of the latest advances in the photographic origination of artwork, in paper science and technology, and in various methods of printing were equally inventive and innovative.

The British forgery of French assignats

Until recently most references to the forgery of assignats in Britain in the 1790s have dismissed the whole thing as a vile slander on the probity and integrity of the English establishment, and have carried some sort of disclaimer dissociating the British government of the day, or the Bank of England, or any members of the establishment, from any knowledge of or involvement in the project. More rarely, the occasional writer has lamented the lack of evidence. Research over the past ten years has uncovered much concrete proof in the form of documentary evidence as well as some of the actual artefacts used. It is now possible to document the whole of this operation from the foremen and workers of the paper mills, through printers, engravers, merchants, pamphleteers, the military, the Court of Directors of the Bank of England, and the Cabinet right up to the Prime Minister and Chancellor of the Exchequer, William Pitt.

Seldom has the introduction and use of any paper currency been the cause of so much suffering and chaos as the French issue of assignats in the years between 1789 and 1795. The internal and external pressures at work in France – the war against Austria, the Terror and the Vendée rebellion – were to produce 13,000% inflation in France by 1795, resulting in the eventual and perhaps inevitable withdrawal of assignats from circulation and the official destruction of the remaining currency, presses and paper stocks.[3] But it was not only these pressures that brought financial chaos to Revolutionary France. Perhaps the biggest single factor was an idea: that of destroying the financial stability and basis of a country by flooding it with forged currency, carried out by a mixture of private enterprise and government. The active participation of agents of the British government was, in many instances, far beyond the authority inherent in their positions.

In November 1789, in order to raise finances and as part of its renunciation of the old feudal order, the National Assembly, the new government of France, nationalised all church lands: a total of some 20,000 square miles, approximately 10% of the country. The idea was originally proposed by the then Bishop of Autun, better known to history as Talleyrand, on 10 October 1789, the day that Louis XVI became King of the French, rather than King of France. He was still on his throne, but only precariously: the people were becoming more powerful.

The sale of these properties, the *Domaines Nationaux*, was to provide the financial base of the new regime, via the issue of interest-bearing bonds, called assignats. Despite warnings from some members of the National Assembly that the release of so much land on to the market would devalue all property prices and thus the value of the assignats, men like Thomas Lindet, the regicide, considered it patriotic to use them. He wrote that:

> Assignats will soon be dispersed all over the country and, in spite of himself, every man who holds them will become a defender of the Revolution.[4]

Whilst it may have been the patriotic thing to do, those who amassed paper fortunes, and indeed, all those who used assignats, were to incur heavy losses. By May 1791 assignats had stopped bearing interest and by the time they were finally withdrawn in 1795, an assignat with a face value of 100 livres was worth no more than 15 sous. John Gamble, an Englishman working in Paris throughout this period who had many connections with paper-making both in France and Britain, wrote in his journal about the paper from the mill owned by his brother-in-law, Leger Didot, at Essonnes near Paris – one of the paper-mills which supplied the government printing houses responsible for issuing assignats:

> The paper was frequently sent in a damp state in covered carts, drawn by post horses to the printing office in Paris, was immediately printed and signed by the proper authorities during the night and as soon as the paper was sufficiently dry it was issued in the morning to the public. I remember the numerous laughs and jokes that took place when Didot returned from Paris with a small bundle of assignats under his arm, which was all that he had received in payment for the many cartloads of paper with which he had supplied the government; the only

Colour plate 1
(*left*) English wood-engraved block for
50 sols assignat, issue
of 4 January 1792. The
genuine assignat was
printed from metal
stereotypes rather than
wooden blocks. (Fuller
Collection, Paleography
Room, University of
London Library)

Colour plate 2
(*below*) Leon Warnerke's
home-made mould for
producing 1890s
100 rouble banknote
paper.

Colour plate 3
(*left*) Pen and ink tracing of the 100 rouble watermark onto transparent celluloid film.

Colour plate 4
(*below*) Two pages from Warnerke's notebook, showing various calculations for the 1890s 100 rouble watermark size on the mould, to take into account the shrinkage of the sheet during drying.

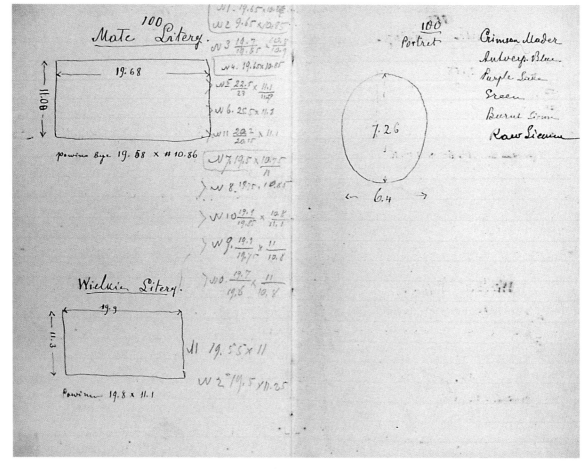

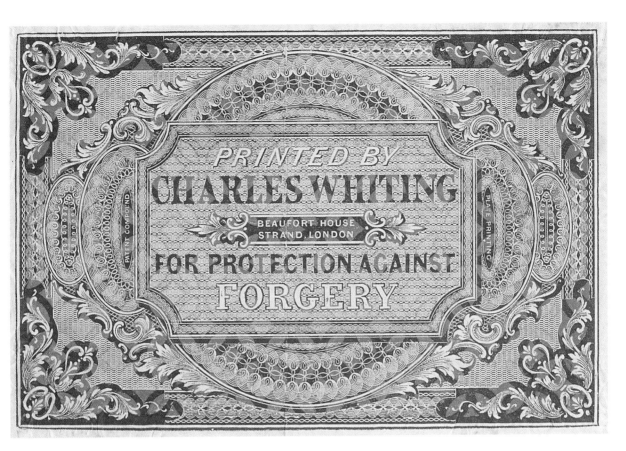

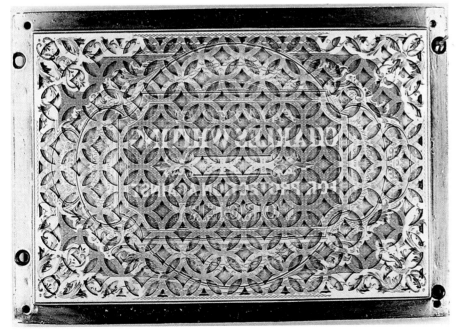

Colour plate 5 (*above*) Charles Whiting's advertisement for compound-plate printing, 1840s.

Colour plate 6 (*left*) Two-part bronze printing plate for Whiting's advertisement.

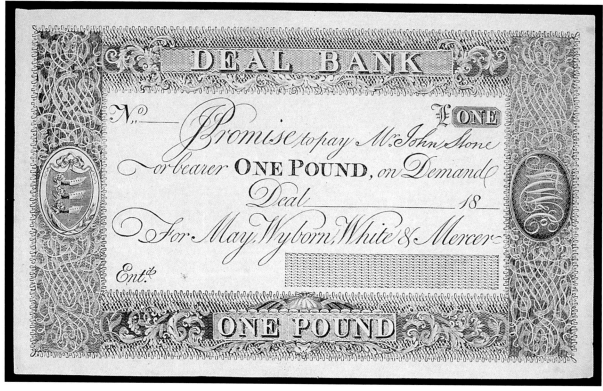

Colour plate 7   Undated colour trial for a £1 note of the Deal Bank.

Colour plate 8   Undated specimen printing for the reverse design of notes from Stuckey's Banking Company, Somersetshire.

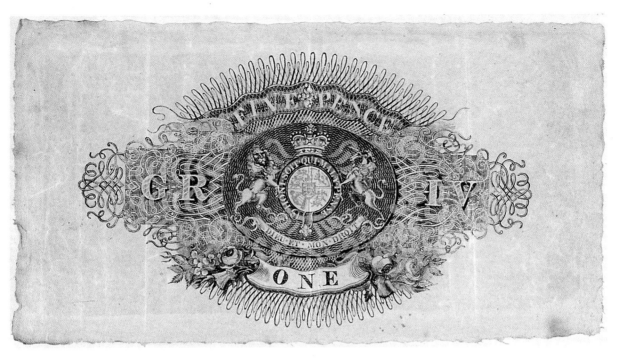

Colour plate 9   Specimen printing of Congreve's duty stamp for £1 notes, 1821.

Colour plate 10   Specimen printing of duty stamp for £1 note, 1823.

Colour plate 11 Forged duty stamp on the reverse of a forged 1 guinea note of the Paisley Banking Company, 1826.

Colour plate 12 Duty stamp for £5 notes, 1826.

Colour plate 13 Forged duty stamp on the reverse of an unissued £5 note of Royd, Smith and Co.'s Rochdale Bank, 1820s.

Colour plate 14
Bank of Spain, 100 pesetas, 30 June
1906, Bradbury, Wilkinson & Co.
(obverse). The two allegorical figures
represent Poetry and Music.

Colour plate 15
Bank of Spain, 100 pesetas, 30 June
1906, Bradbury, Wilkinson & Co.
(reverse).

Colour plate 16
Bank of Spain, 100 pesetas, 15 July
1907, Bradbury, Wilkinson & Co.
(reverse). The building is Seville
Cathedral.

Colour plate 17   Bank of Spain, 100 pesetas, 1 July 1925, Bradbury, Wilkinson & Co. (obverse), with a portrait of Philip II from a painting by Titian and a view of the monastery of El Escorial.

Colour plate 18   Bank of Spain, 50 pesetas, 22 July 1935, Thomas De La Rue (obverse), with a portrait of Santiago Ramón y Cajal (1852–1934), winner of the 1906 Nobel Prize for Medicine.

difference was that when they came back with Didot they had been printed and signed by some of the revolutionary demagogues then at the head of the government. The fate of the assignats is well known. I recollect being in Paris during the time they were ordered to be burnt, and I saw their fragments flying over the heads of thousands of persons who had been utterly ruined by their introduction.[5]

Printing the paper before the sheets were properly dry gives a good idea of the urgency of the French authorities' need for currency. Paper would normally have been dried and cured before leaving the mill. Once at the printers it would have been acclimatised to the workshop conditions before being dampened prior to printing. This series of processes gives a more stable sheet.

The rapid and increasing inflation in France was partly due to a massive over-issue of the new currency. For instance, in 1792 alone, for just one denomination of note, some four million assignats with a face value of 400 livres each were issued. But another more subtle and pernicious threat to the stability of both the currency and the country was the deliberate forging of assignats. This involved not only attempts by private individuals, who in many cases met the extreme penalty, printed on every note – 'La Loi punit de mort le contrefacteur' – and travelled in the tumbrels to the guillotine,[6] but most effectively, the controlled and political use of forgery, by foreign governments and *émigré* leaders, as a deliberate weapon to bring a nation to defeat.

The royal courts of Europe, already alarmed by the events in France since 1789, were outraged by the execution of the king in January 1793. Soon most of Europe would be at war with the fledgling Republic, but the Revolution was defiant: 'The Kings in alliance try to intimidate us', cried Danton. 'We hurl at their feet, as a gage of battle, the French King's head!'[7] Such confidence had only a shaky foundation. The rising cost of living, the declining value of the currency, and long-term shortages of food in some areas all led to increasing unrest, particularly in regions like the Vendée, where the peasants rose against the Paris regime.

The British government and *émigré* leaders, such as the dead king's brother, the Comte d'Artois in England, and Calonne, based in Coblentz, set out to destroy the financial basis of the Revolution. Artois, later Charles X, King of France and Navarre after the Restoration, but then in exile in England, was directly involved in the production of counterfeit assignats. On several occasions, he visited the paper-maker Charles Ball at Albury Park Mill, Surrey, to order new paper, supervise the manufacture of new assignat watermarks and to take delivery of completed paper. On one such visit he became perhaps more involved than he might have wished:

On one occasion he [the Comte d'Artois] required various changes to be made in the watermarks. The 'form-maker' [maker of paper-moulds and watermarks] of the mill was sent for. He was a young man named Longhelt, a native of Germany . . . [it] was explained to him the alteration he wanted to be made, and [Artois] sat down by his side for the purpose of seeing him begin his labour. Longhelt, who had been drinking, resented the intrusion and getting impatient at this stranger's interventions he waxed furious and threw the mould at the visitor's head.[8]

Forging assignats outside France, where French law had no means of tracing, catching or punishing the counterfeiters, was to prove very effective. Sir John Swinburne, who at this time investigated the part played by the British government in what he called 'this scandalous business', wrote:

> In the years 1793 and 1794, Government, Mr Pitt being Minister, caused an immense number of assignats of various values to be fabricated in England, and a prodigious quantity was poured into France ... from Flanders and from the coast of Brittany for the rebels in La Vendée.[9]

Paper for these assignats was produced for the British government by William Smith at Haughton Castle Mill, Northumberland (fig. 1), and by John Finch at Dartford, Kent. Paper for the *émigrés* was made by Charles Ball at Albury Park Mill, Surrey.[10] The foreman at Haughton Mill told Swinburne that:

> they had had for this paper very great orders and for several months they had made nothing else, sometimes ninety reams of different kinds per week, that were sent to Mr Watson the partner in London, every week, often by the mail coach.[11]

The 'Mr Watson' mentioned is Sir Brook Watson, one of the Directors of the Bank of England, who had considerable business interests and a paper warehouse in Lambeth – used for making 'fancy' decorated paper – to which the Haughton Castle paper was transported. Sending paper by the mail coach, particularly in such large amounts, was a very expensive way of transporting it, but faster and much more 'secure' than more usual methods.

The watermarked moulds, for forming the sheets, were sent from London 'frequently of course, when any change was made in the paper in France'. The French authorities went to extraordinary lengths to defeat the forgers and the developments in paper and printing technology made at this time were to have a great effect on both industries. Two of the moulds used by William Smith at Haughton Castle Mill still survive in the possession of the Newcastle Society of Antiquities (fig. 2). Both are in a very damaged state, but enough remains of the light and shade impressions in the wire and the raised wiremarks to identify their original purpose.[12] Eight unprinted paper samples from Haughton Castle Mill, destined for five different assignat issues, have also survived (fig. 3).[13]

Engravers were employed to make the blocks: even Thomas Bewick, renowned for his wood engravings of wildlife and nature, and who engraved plates for various English provincial banks, was asked to make assignat plates 'that might be cut very sharp, as a very great number of impressions would be wanted'. According to Swinburne, Bewick 'very honourably declined, he would have no part in such business'.[14] Although the French originals were printed using a stereotype process,[15] at least some of the English forgeries were printed from engraved wood blocks and are thus relatively easy to distinguish. One such block has recently been discovered amongst some uncatalogued wood blocks, and impressions taken from it compare very accurately with examples of forgeries recognised at the time by the French authorities (col. plate 1).[16]

The duplicity of the British government and its agents was extraordinary. A printer, Strongitharm, had been commissioned by the London stationer William Lukyn, acting for the government, to print a run of assignats. Lukyn, wanting to keep the government's money for himself, tried to get out of paying him by saying that as Strongitharm was forging and forging was illegal, then they did not have to pay him. Strongitharm courageously took the case to court and won, Lord Kenyon's judgement being that as the assignats 'were circulated by the authority of the higher powers of this country . . . the plaintiff was entitled to recover'.[17]

The finished notes were transported to France via two routes. One was with the British Expeditionary Force in Flanders, directly involving the British military at the highest level. The second was via a base in Jersey, used particularly on the *émigré* invasion of Brittany in 1794. One extraordinary story from the Flanders end of the operation involves an Englishman, John Barton, who had been living in France for many years before the Revolution. He had lived on the income from moneys invested in French government funds which had been left to him as a young man. On the declaration of war between England and France in 1793 these funds were confiscated and he

> obtained for some time a precarious livelihood from the liberality of friends, being preserved from the inconveniences of personal restraint from having acquired such a perfect French accent, that the authorities did not discover his English Origin.[18]

Eventually he found a job as an inspector of assignats at Delft in Holland, then under French control. Part of his work involved tracking the shipments of forged assignats from Britain. The Kent antiquarian John Dunkin, who knew Barton well, describes his later life:

> In 1799, seeing no prospect of any termination to the war, he resigned his situation as Inspector, and took up his residence in the neighbourhood of Calais, from whence, after many years absence, in which he had lost the idiom of his native tongue and had been nearly forgotten by his kindred, he escaped with several English *détenus*, in an open boat to Dover, where he landed without money, with no other property than the clothes he wore.[19]

Barton settled in Dartford near the paper-maker John Finch, who had been involved in producing the false assignat paper:

> The self acknowledged forger of the spurious paper and its once anxious detector, in the decline of their days, resided within a few doors of each other, and oft times convivially spent their evenings together, where the writer [John Dunkin] has often heard the former detail the narrow escape he once had from the latter, whilst accompanying a convoy of several chests full of the base money through the Black Forest, where the chase becoming too hot, they were eventually buried. To add still more to the coincidences, the immediate previous occupant (Mills) of the apartment wherein Mr Barton breathed his last was an apprentice in the very

printing office in London where the forged assignats were printed and he too had actually been engaged in this dishonest and discreditable work.[20]

By 1795, when assignats were withdrawn from circulation, the economic plight of France was disastrous. 2,400,000 livres of a new paper currency, *Mandats Territoriaux*, were issued, but these depreciated so rapidly that by early 1797, when they were withdrawn, they were only worth 1% of their face value. Beggars would not take them and peasants wanted metal coin for their produce, saying that they would only take 'the other stuff' if their horses would eat it. An anonymous rhyme, reputed to come from the eighteenth century, ironically highlights the connections between paper money, poverty and paper-making:

Rags make Paper
Paper makes Money
Money makes Banks
Banks make Loans
Loans make Beggars
Beggars make Rags.

Leon Warnerke (1837–1900), master forger

In 1991 a remarkable collection of banknotes, printing trials, watermarks, paper-making moulds, letters, receipts, Memorandum book, photographic material, press cuttings, and ink trials was brought to my attention.[21] Examination of this complex material has revealed an extraordinary story. Until recently the accepted biography of Leon Warnerke ran as follows. In 1871 a wealthy young man, with his wife and young daughter, arrived in London from Paris. Over the years he established himself as a very successful businessman and inventor dealing with the technology of photography, winning prizes and awards and enjoying the respect of his peers. Although based for most of the latter part of his life in a large imposing house on Champion Hill, in south-east London, his business and photographic interests led him to travel constantly throughout Europe. He died in Geneva in October 1900 (fig. 4).[22]

However, the mass of documents which surfaced in 1991 tells a very different story, suggesting that this well-respected man had another life: for some thirty years he was also involved in forging the banknotes of Russia and other countries,[23] as part of a widespread conspiracy that grew out of an alliance of survivors of the Paris Commune, anarchists, Polish exiles and rebels fighting the Russian influence in their country, and gangsters out for what they could get.

The whole question of Warnerke's true identity and the part he played in this grand conspiracy is a complex and multifaceted problem. His public persona is briefly documented in various sources, which give a particular image of a man of singular talent and character.[24] Leon Warnerke was born, by his own description, in Moravia, then one of the provinces of the Austro-Hungarian Empire. His entry in the 1881 census places him at 'Silvenhall', Champion Hill, Camberwell and lists him as

Austrian.[25] His return for the 1891 census, at the same address, this time spelt 'Silverhowe House', Champion Hill, Camberwell, lists his place of birth as Moravia, Austria.[26] In both these returns there are considerable discrepancies between the entries for all the members of the Warnerke family.[27]

The historian of photography Joseph Eder was convinced that Warnerke was Russian by birth on the basis of conversations with his (Eder's) collaborator, Joseph Plener, who had also worked with Warnerke in London.[28] Eder says that:

> Joseph Plener convinced this author that Warnerke was a Russian by Birth. Plener was a Pole in Czarist Russia and at that time involved in a Revolt against Russia. He fled to London as a Russian emigrant. He devoted himself to photography . . . In London, Plener had close personal contact with Warnerke, with whom he was able to converse in Russian, his mother tongue, and he always described Warnerke as a Russian.[29]

The mystery of Warnerke's origin is further compounded by examination of the letters. These documents, consisting of actual letters, draft letters and copies of letters made by Warnerke, his wife Marie, and other hands, date from the 1860s to the late 1890s and are to and from several different people. The letters are in English, French, Polish and Russian, and sometimes in a mixture of these languages.

Amongst a whole series of letters relating to a court case, one in particular is of interest. It is sent to Marie, Warnerke's wife, from Nicolai Pogolski, a one-time friend and co-conspirator of Warnerke, who sometimes stayed with them at Champion Hill.[30] By 1897 Pogolski and Warnerke were no longer friends, and the court case was an acrimonious affair, involving blackmail. This letter from Pogolski sheds much light on various groups of documents relating to a certain Wladyslaw Malachowski, which had previously been difficult to intepret. He writes to Marie Warnerke in Polish, accusing Warnerke of having several aliases:

9th November 1897

> Most respected Lady
>
> Enough of this!! This comedy makes us a laughing stock, diminishes us in the eyes of foreigners. I will bring this comedy to an end. At this moment I am busy preparing three documents, one for the Judge, one for the lawyer and the third will be lying on my desk. In each one I mention everybody, beginning with Wladyslaw Malachowski, alias Fr. Schultz from Tor. Av.; alias Fr. Wolf from Springfield Ter, alias Warnerke of Silverhowe etc one after the other.

One of these 'aliases', Wladyslaw Malachowski, was already familiar to me from reading some of the earlier letters: a series in Polish dating from the late 1860s to early 1870s, from a Josef Horodice to Wladyslaw Malachowski. Some of this series contain references to the organisation of the network in which Warnerke and others were involved, and cryptic references to codes, invisible inks, and a range of complex communications procedures to be followed by the conspirators.

There are many other Malachowski family documents, including *The Last Will and Testament of Julian Simon Malachowski*, Wladyslaw's father, dated 26 April 1865. There are also repeated references in Warnerke's own letters to obtaining his father's family papers, including land grants and the details of various properties in Poland. But the political situation, the Russianisation of that part of Poland where the family estates lay, now Byelorus, and the uprisings by the Poles against the Russian occupation, made it very difficult for Warnerke/Malachowski to claim his inheritance. Wladyslaw, like Joseph Plener, mentioned earlier, had to flee into exile, but unlike his friend, he had felt it better to make a new identity for himself – an identity which might then have been compromised by claiming his inheritance.

The problems of communication between the conspirators were immense. Amongst the mass of documentation in this collection there are groups of letters which clearly relate to each other, and some of these pieces give an extraordinary insight into the risks faced by some of those involved in the scheme. One such group, consisting of drafts for coded letters, invisible ink letters and a press clipping, all refer to the arrest of a certain Josephine Dobrovolska on the Polish/Russian border.[31]

The press clipping, two copies of which were tucked into a notebook perhaps sent to Warnerke by colleagues on the continent, is from an undated, unnamed French-language newspaper. The notebook contains many such cuttings, in English, French, Polish and Russian, all referring to the forging of banknotes and covering quite a long period of time. The Polish and Russian articles were primarily concerned with warning the public of the specific details of various forged notes, whilst the French and English are somewhat more general, talking in terms of the threat to economic stability posed by such anarchistic projects.[32]

The precise role of many of the individuals mentioned by name in the mass of Warnerke documents is often obscure. But in the case of these examples we have some specific information. A courier, Josephine Dobrovolska, was arrested at the Wierzbolowo customs post on the Polish/Russian border. According to the newspaper, she was carrying 20,800 roubles in false 10 and 50 rouble notes. It is interesting to compare this figure with that given in one of the letters from her companion who managed to escape arrest, where she is described as having only 15,810 roubles. This letter, written in invisible ink under a perfectly innocuous covering letter and then treated by the recipient to make it legible (fig. 5), is essentially an appeal for funds, the writer asking for money to be sent to him so that he can stay free.[33] The use of invisible ink seems to have been common at least in the early stages of this giant conspiracy. There are other examples in different hands, and also examples where letters have been tested to see if such invisible messages are present. Another letter actually talks of preparing the paper and is perhaps worth quoting in full for the light it sheds on the organisation:

2nd September

My dear Sir

Although we still haven't received any letters from Max[34] – Don't forget that he has left here under the impression that our position is possibly dangerous. It would be best to reassure him. And as Jos.[35] is aware that we will use the new ink it is necessary that you prepare the paper. It seems to me that the best means of despatch would be by [indecipherable] Send him the address today in invisible ink and coded. He will address the letter to himself. [crossed out: Ask Madame to write a smokescreen of a letter in French.] When you have the paper ready send it to us with the smokescreen of what you want to say. Don't forget to write to us.

H . . .[36]

Unfortunately most of these letters, and most of the drafts, are undated but this one appears to belong to a group dating from the 1870s. Trying to date the arrest of Dobrovolska is a little difficult. But a possible answer lies in eight pages (on two sheets) of draft letters written to different people in different languages. One of these letters, written in a blend of Polish and Russian, contains references to Dobrovolska and her arrest; another gives information about the man who wrote the group of letters written in invisible ink referred to above. Others are dated 1872 and 1873, so it is at least possible that the Dobrovolska arrest dates from then. Besides the different languages, there are code-names for some of the conspirators, details of arrangements and, perhaps most interestingly, many words have been given a number code. There are some indications that 'one-off' codes may have been in use as the numbering of the letters in this group of draft letters does not relate to the code key grids which were also found in the collection. It is obvious that communication between the various people involved was a major problem, and judging by the amount of travelling referred to, particularly for Max and another man named Turc (possibly the same person, known to different members of the conspiracy under different names), probably more efficiently undertaken person to person, despite the dangers, rather than through the mails.

Some of the connections between the people involved continued for many years. In the correspondence from the late 1890s relating to the blackmail case, we find a certain Josef talked of constantly in a series of draft letters, in a hand that is as yet difficult to identify, written in response to Pogolski's letters. This suggests that Pogolski itself may be an alias. These letters seem to be calling Pogolski 'Josef', possibly the Joseph Horodice or Horodynski who was writing letters, or is mentioned in letters, as early as the 1860s. We also find Nicolai Pogolski writing to the Princess Oginska in 1897, a woman mentioned in the French press clipping as being involved in the transfer of forged roubles as early as Dobrovolska's arrest early in the 1870s.

Resolving all the riddles posed by these letters, where every discovery prompts new questions, will be a painstaking task, but with careful translation and analysis they should reveal more of the extraordinarily complex lives of those involved. Perhaps the most fascinating part of the collection, however, is the banknotes and of these the most intriguing are the counterfeits of the 1866 10 rouble issue. Many were printed on English-made paper watermarked J WHATMAN, but they also contain the normal lined and patterned 10 rouble mark. Close examination of the two marks show that the J WHATMAN mark is on the wire side of the sheet, as one would expect in a handmade sheet. The style and scale of the letter forms visible suggest that this

WHATMAN sheet was made by W. & R. Balston at Springfield Mill, Kent. Balstons were supplying Russia with some handmade writing papers in the nineteenth century, but never banknote paper. The real curiosity lies in the relationship between the two watermarks. The Russian mark is on the opposite (felt) side. No paper-making process, then or now, allows watermarking from two sides of the sheet.

There is, however, an explanation for this apparent conundrum: a friend and colleague of Warnerke, who sat on various Royal Photographic Society committees with him, and who lived nearby in Camberwell, was Walter Woodbury,[37] inventor of the 'Woodburytype' method of reproducing photographs. Woodbury also developed a further refinement of his technique which he called 'photo-filigrane'. Woodbury's technique used a relief of hardened gelatine in which the lights and shades of any photograph were reproduced by varying the thicknesses of the gelatine. When such a gelatine film was placed in contact with a sheet of already made paper and the two were subjected to very heavy pressure, the paper was more impressed where the gelatine was thicker, and less impressed where it was thinner, thus producing a picture, on first impression exactly like a watermark.[38] It is possible that Warnerke, who well understood the properties of gelatine, paper and the techniques of photography, adapted or utilised his own version of Woodbury's technique for the watermarks in some of the earlier forgeries, although he was later to depend on making up true watermarks on moulds.

Warnerke's methods changed considerably throughout his working life and the curious blend of amateurish but inspired improvisation and complex technological sophistication becomes more and more marked as one examines the various trials, proofs, essays and finished products, particularly towards the end of his working life. Warnerke's use of a version of Woodbury's photo-filigrane process, probably whilst Woodbury himself was developing it from his Woodburytype photographic engraving process, is a measure of his familiarity with the most up-to-date methods and techniques, and a measure of his imaginative use of anything that might further his purpose, whatever the source.

The extent of his knowledge is quite extraordinary, ranging from photography to paper-making, watermarking and printing. One of his special areas of knowledge, essential to anyone wishing to forge the banknotes of the period, was the use and preparation of the gelatine used for sizing the sheets of paper. In a report on a lecture, given by Thomas Bolas as part of the Bolt Court series,[39] we find the chairman asking Warnerke to round the meeting off by describing a method of purifying gelatine that Warnerke had recently tested:

> Mr Warnerke said that the method in question consisted of making a solution of gelatine or glue in hot water, to which was added alum in excess, which would cause the gelatine to precipitate. In this state it could be thoroughly washed in hot water, after which it was strained out and a little citric acid added. This rendered the gelatine again soluble. The next step was to allow the gelatine to set, and to wash it in cold water to remove the excess of citric acid. The final result would be a gelatine of very considerable purity.[40]

Warnerke was a frequent visitor to such meetings throughout his life and as an article about him states:

> Mr Warnerke is of the most sociable and genial disposition, and ever ready to assist by his advice or otherwise, in any matters photographic; and few of the regular frequenters of the meetings of the metropolitan photographic societies, or of those who have enjoyed his hospitality, but have cause to be grateful for his kind assistance in some photographic difficulty.[41]

One area where the blend of amateur ingenuity and sophisticated professional techniques can clearly be seen is in the construction and employment of the mould and watermark for the 1890s 100 rouble note (col. plate 2). The watermark has been traced directly from a genuine note onto a celluloid film using pen and ink (col. plate 3). Warnerke was, however, well aware that all paper shrinks as it dries and when he constructed the watermark on the mould's surface he had to take this shrinkage into account. The notebook found amongst Warnerke's papers shows several examples of such calculations (col. plate 4). Comparisons of the handwriting identified as Warnerke's in some of the letters with the writing in this notebook shows that these calculations were all made by Warnerke. They were absolutely crucial to the success of the counterfeiting of this particular issue as the printed image on the back of the note had to align precisely with various parts of the watermark.

The actual method of watermark construction is of great interest. Rather than using bent and soldered wire as would have been normal, Warnerke employed what appears to be an enamel paint, building it up in layers and then carving it down to the correct shape. This would have been a most laborious process, but had the advantage of allowing very fine adjustments to the actual form of the watermark by the addition or subtraction of minute amounts of the enamel. In complete contrast to this work is the watermark used for the 1866 50 rouble note, which on close examination in the sheet shows every indication of having been produced by wires and by the raising and lowering of the three oval or circular areas of the wire. The mould for this note has unfortunately not survived. This use of different levels of wire can also be seen on the forming surface of the 100 rouble mould.

The very high quality of this particular note, and the 10 and 25 rouble notes from the same period, suggest that at least at some periods in his career as a banknote forger Warnerke had access to highly experienced paper-makers and to the necessary equipment and raw materials, if not to genuine material as well. Joseph Eder's account of Warnerke's time in St Petersburg suggests just such a possible connection during the early 1880s, through the Imperial Russian Office for the Production of Government Papers.[42] According to Eder, Leon Warnerke was born in 1837 in Russia. He was a civil engineer, but devoted himself entirely to photography. He spent his youth in St Petersburg and came to London in 1870, where he started a private photochemical laboratory and invented the roll holder with silver bromide collodion stripping-paper. He worked a great deal with silver bromide collodion, received a prize from Belgium in 1877 for his work in this field, and in 1881 the Progress Medal of the Royal Photographic Society of Great Britain. He gave lectures before the photographic societies of England, France, Belgium and Germany. In 1880 he founded, at St Petersburg, a photographic firm and a technical journal. He also had financial interests in the manufacture of dry plates in Russia. The first Russian gelatine dry-plate factory was erected by A. Felisch in 1881. Then Warnerke, with Stresnowsky, established a gelatine silver bromide plate factory in St Petersburg, to which he later added the manufacture of gelatine silver chloride papers.

The tempestuous political conditions during this period of Tsarist rule and the large amount of propaganda material, printed mostly in underground printing shops, caused the most rigorous supervision of all printing presses by the government, which was a great hindrance to the spread of the techniques of reproduction:

> Official photography was advanced especially by the Imperial Russian Technical Society in St Petersburg, which consisted of several sections, each of which dealt with one of the different technical fields as its subject proper. Urged by Warnerke, the fifth group of the Society, 'The Photographic Section', was established in 1880. It became the important centre of the photographic industry and of the various branches of industrial, artistic and scientific photography. From here we published the Reports of the 'Office for the Production of Government Papers', St Petersburg, and of the cartographic section of the Central Staff, which had in its service studios and efficient reproduction technicians.[43]

The Imperial Russian Office for the Production of Government Papers was responsible for the production of bonds, rouble notes, stock certificates and valuable printed matter of all sorts. This appears to be Warnerke's connection with the official production of Russian banknotes, but further work needs to be done to resolve this question.

The painstaking accuracy for which Warnerke strived is well illustrated by the large numbers of photographic negatives and positive prints also found in this collection. Many of these bear the marks of additional alterations and working out of specific details by hand. He also spent considerable time and effort to achieve the correct balance of inks for the 100 rouble rainbow-tinted note, listing in more than one place in his notebook the specific colours necessary. The annotation of these colour trial sheets in English, with the names of artists' colourmen working in London, suggests that at least the trials and proofing were being done in England. The colours on one sheet bear names of makers such as *J Winston Bronze 1893*, *Millar Blue* and *Stanbury 1893*, but most of the colours are merely labelled with their names. There is evidence in some of the letters that work was also being done in France and Poland, but the heart of the conspiracy was here in England, in a large and comfortable private house in a quiet and secluded road in Camberwell, where a very civilised and popular gentleman, well respected by his friends and neighbours, lived an extra-ordinary double life.

Acknowledgements

All research depends on collaboration and many people have assisted me in the unravelling of both the assignat and the Warnerke stories. I would especially like to thank Iain Bain, Susy Bioletti, Gerald Bowden, Dave Carter, Alan Crocker, Ranson Davey, Jack Gilbey of Whatman Ltd, Mike Grey, Curator of the Fox Talbot Museum, Peter Isaac, Colin Narbeth, Michael O'Grady, John Phillipson, Dr Christopher Pond, Kate Rouse, Assistant Curator of the Royal Photographic Society, Nicola Smith of Southwark Local History Library, Pekka Viljannen, Brenda Weedon of the University of London Library, Maria Woods, and the staffs of Swiss Cottage Library, the Newspaper Library (Cricklewood), the British Library, the British Museum, the Public Record Office, the Probate Office, and the Bar Library at the High Court. I would also particularly like to thank Sally Bower, Elizabeth Einberg and Kasia Szeleynski for their help with translating and interpreting the Warnerke documents and letters, and Marcus Leith and Richard Kindersley for their help with photography.

Notes

1. Both these stories are the subjects of individual books currently in preparation.

2. As late as 1852 Napoleon's grandson, the emperor Napoleon III, was paying a pension to Mlle de Montant, the daughter of the engraver involved in this particular project, to ensure her silence over his predecessor's activities.

3. In fact much important material survived, primarily due to the efforts of Armand Gaston Camus, Guardian of the Archives of the Republic. This material consists of drawings, proofs, preparatory designs, documentation, notes themselves, stereotypes, paper-making moulds, clishes, etc. In addition to material in private hands, the most important material can be found in three collections: the Conservatoire National des Arts et Metiers (CNAM) in the Musée National des Technologies; the Archives Nationales, held in the Musée de l'Histoire de France; and the Hotel de la Monnaie de Paris. Some of this material is illustrated and discussed in Alain Mercier's *L'Argent des Révolutionnaires*, Paris 1989. Camus himself documented some of the details of assignat production in his *Histoire et Procédés du Polytypage et du Stéréotypage*, published in Paris in 1802.

4. Hibbert, Christopher, *The French Revolution*, London 1980, p. 110.

5. The original document is in the Public Record Office but this quotation comes from Clapperton, R.H., *The Paper-making Machine*, Oxford 1967, p. 23.

6. Over 1,300 individuals were convicted of counterfeiting assignats and met their deaths on the guillotine.

7. Hibbert, op. cit., p. 193.

8. Charles Ashby Ball, the grandson of Charles Ball, who as a child was present when these events took place, recalling them in *The Stationer and Fancy Trades' Register* of 5 April 1869, p. 196.

9. Swinburne, Sir John, MS Memorandum in the Northumberland County Record Office, ZSW 590.

10. The possibility that Langley Mill, Durham, was also used for the government project is still being researched.

11. Swinburne, op. cit.

12. Now in the Museum of Science and Industry, Newcastle-upon-Tyne. Mould 1938.6 and Mould 1938.7.

13. a) 2 examples 50 Sols assignat, Emission décrétée Le 4 Janvier 1792 (see also note 16);
b) 1 example 10 Livres assignat, Emission décrétée Le 24 Octobre 1792;
c) 1 example 50 Livres assignat, Emission décrétée Le 23 Mai 1793;
d) 3 examples 50 Sols assignat, Emission décrétée Le 6 Juin 1793.
Catalogued with the Swinburne Memorandum, Northumberland County Record Office, ZSW 590.

14. Swinburne, op. cit.

15. Camus, op. cit.

16. Wood-engraved block used for printing 50 Sols assignat, Emission décrétée Le 4 Janvier 1792 (see note 13). Fuller Collection, Paleography Library, University of London Library.

17. *Espinasse's Reports*, Strongitharm v Lukyn. 36 George III 1795, pp. 388–91.

18. Dunkin, John, *The History and Antiquities of Dartford*, 1844, p. 233.

19. Dunkin, op. cit.

20. Dunkin, op. cit.

21. Offered at auction at Phillips, London, Friday 4 October 1991, Lot 277, and now in a private collection. Written up for Phillips: Bower,

Report No. 29 91 15. Further information written up for the present owner in Bower, Report No. 47 92 11.

22. Eder, Joseph Maria, *History of Photography*, translated by Edward Epstean, New York 1945, p. 452. There is however some doubt as to whether he did actually die in Geneva as Eder states. Further work needs to be done to resolve this question.

23. There is evidence that the forgery of both French and British banknotes were also part of this widespread conspiracy, but in this paper I will concentrate on the Russian material.

24. Jones, Bernard, *Cyclopaedia of Photography*, nd. p. 559, *The British Journal of Photography*, 18 January 1884, p. 39 and *The British Journal Photographic Almanac*, 1901, p. 672 all list Warnerke as being of Hungarian origin. This is not inconsistent with Warnerke's description of himself, as Moravia was then part of the Austro-Hungarian Empire.

25. Public Record Office: 1881 Census Records. RG11/674.

26. Public Record Office: 1891 Census Records. RG12/466.

27. For example, Warnerke's wife Marie, who was 45 in 1881, is only 52 in 1891, having lost three years, whilst Sophie has lost two years, going from 12 years old in 1881 to 20 in 1891. Marie had originally given her place of birth as Belgium and Sophie's as France, but by 1891 they are both registered as having been born in Austria.

28. Eder, op. cit., p. 451.

29. Eder, op. cit. p. 782, note 2.

30. The 1891 census places a Nicolas Pogolsky as a 'visitor' in the house on the census date, and describes him as 'living on own means' and as having been born in 'Russia S Petersburg'.

31. Josephine Dobrovolska was a survivor of the Paris Commune.

32. For example, a French language clipping, dated 20 April 1897, subtitled 'une nouvelle manoeuvre anarchiste', describes a massive plot to undermine the economies of France, Belgium, Germany and Russia.

33. This letter is part of a group of letters all unsigned and undated and all written in invisible ink by the same hand. They all appear to come from the same period, are all written on the same paper, and all have been given the same chemical preparation and late treatment.

34. Max (or Maj) is frequently mentioned in several letters. He appears to have been travelling Europe under an assumed name.

35. Possibly Joseph Horodice.

36. The signature is very difficult to decipher, possibly Herve.

37. Walter Woodbury (1834–85) was a well-travelled and inventive man. During his younger years he lived in both Australia and Java before returning to his birthplace, England, in 1863. Between 1866 and his death nineteen years later he took out over twenty patents for photochemical printing processes and for photographic and allied apparatus. He died suddenly at Margate in 1885 from the effects of an overdose of laudanum. Examples of his work can be seen in Bower, Peter, 'Walter Woodbury and The Photo-Filigrane Process', in *The Quarterly*, the Journal of the British Association of Paper Historians, no. 12, September 1994, pp. 10–12.

38. Richard Brown, of Brown, Barnes & Bell, working independently of Woodbury, also devised and patented a similar photo-filigrane process but ran into a little trouble with the police when he tried to persuade the Bank of England to buy up and suppress his method on the grounds that it would facilitate forgery.

39. Thomas Bolas gave the fourth Bolt Court lecture on *Gelatine as the leading Colloid for Process work – Compounds of Chromium*. The Bolt Court School later became part of the London College of Printing, now the London Institute.

40. *The Process Photogram & Illustrator*, no. 54, June 1898, pp. 87–9.

41. *The British Journal of Photography*, 18 January 1884, p. 39.

42. Eder, op. cit., pp. 451–2 and 708–10.

43. Eder, ibid.

1 Haughton Castle Mill, Northumberland, where the paper for at least five issues of counterfeit assignats was produced. (Photo: Ranson Davey)

2 Papermaking mould used at Haughton Mill, Northumberland, in *c.* 1793–5 for the production of 200 livres assignats, issue of 7 Vendémiaire Year 2. The remains of the watermark pattern and a date can be seen. (Society of Antiquaries of Newcastle upon Tyne, 1938.7)

3 (*above*) Beta-radiograph of an unprinted sheet
made at Haughton Mill, Northumberland, in
1793 or 1794. This paper was intended for the
production of copies of the 50 livres assignat,
issued on 14 December 1792. (Northumberland
County Record Office, ZSW 590)

4 (*right*) Portrait of Leon Warnerke, from the
Supplement to the *British Journal of
Photography*, 18 January 1884.

5 (*opposite*) Letter written in invisible ink
describing the arrest of Josephine Dobrovolska.
Two sets of writing can be seen. The fainter
lines are the letter that was written on top of
the hidden message. After chemical treatment
the true message appears darker and the
ordinary words fade away. (Ultra-violet
photograph by Marcus Leith)

Kochana Pani niech Bóg wynagrodzi
najpiękniejszy list otrzymałem w mojej od
Kobiékiów że esffach Bóg daje Pani mnie
przysłała mnie w potrzebnych czas
....y zwianem bez chleba byłem
bo mnie nie pozwolono ni co ja...
najpierwsze nie na ...
wierzchał ...
dla niewiększej ...... Mój dopus..
taki że niewiem nic dlacziar..
orzyli mnie jej że dopuszy w
....
niewiadoma ... bo bardzo trudn..
dowiedziéé się na Za do mnie Pani
w gazety pisana dalto że ono ...
.... pispieszy od Pani do doma
wiémiá do Wólna w Hotel Kr..
...... Wilhelminie pod N. 5
piérwéj pisano że wniej było
15, i 10 od kroj ...... Kamińki ...
dwenny czy nowajik Płońske
i Zgamalow podonosie na
nie na Pani ja bej osobą

6

A case study: classifying the notes of the Hongkong and Shanghai Bank Corporation, 1865–1898

Joe Cribb

The origins of this paper go back to 1986 when I was asked to write an illustrated introduction to the money collection of The Hongkong and Shanghai Bank. The main part of the collection was the paper money issues of the Bank itself. From its foundation in 1865 down to the present day The Hongkong and Shanghai Bank has been the most important issuer of paper money in Hong Kong. In the past it also issued paper money at its branches in China, Japan and Malaya. The collection was large but, armed with a typed catalogue of the notes (supplied by the Bank's Archive Department) and a set of photocopies of the collection (provided by William Barrett), I set about trying to understand the history of the Bank's activities as an issuer of paper money sufficiently well to write about it.

My first response was to look for publications on the subject. I found little to help me: a brief essay on some unusual issues of the Bank by Judith Sear, and catalogue listings by Smith and Maltravers, Mao, Lam and in Pick's *Standard Catalog of World Paper Money*. Sear's article mentioned only two notes relevant to the topic of this paper, both exceptional pieces (one a Hong Kong note of 1865 issued at the Yokohama branch in 1866; the other a trial note made by a printer tendering for the Bank's business in 1888, both in the Bank's collection), which are useful evidence for the story of the Bank's note issue during the period in question, but not part of it. Mao's *History* consisted of lengthy but unhelpful descriptions of badly illustrated notes (a few not listed elsewhere), with occasional paragraphs of uninformative comment. The catalogue listings by Smith, Pick and Lam contained useful data, brief descriptions and a few illustrations, but did not provide a clear account of the process of note issue. They all recorded the notes seen by their authors in denomination and date order, but offered no solutions to the task awaiting me.

It seemed to me that I had to go back to basics, so I added the material published by Mao, Smith, Pick and Lam to what I knew from the Bank's collection and started to examine the notes to see what they had to show. I was also able to add to my material photocopies of the notes in a substantial private collection (William Barrett's). In this way I assembled details of a large number of notes issued by the Bank, and it was from these notes themselves, together with some documentary evidence made available to me by the Bank and by the same collector, that I acquired the information I needed to reconstruct an overview of the production and issue of The Hongkong and Shanghai Bank's paper money. For the purposes of this article I am confining myself to the note issues from the Bank's Hong Kong Branch during the period 1865 to 1898, with the exception of the $1 notes issued from 1872, as they are worthy of a paper to themselves (which I hope to present on a future occasion).

I have chosen to describe the methods I used in classifying these notes in order to demonstrate the value of classification as a core tool in the study of paper money, which can be employed as a means of understanding the history of the notes themselves, the history of the issuing bank and its monetary activities, and the history of banknote production. The bare bones of my classification are those used in all catalogue listings, best exemplified by those of Pick and Lam, but the intention is to go deeper into the criteria for classification in order to produce not just a guide for collecting and valuing notes, but a framework which will elucidate the importance of the information contained in the notes, which are historical documents in their own right.

Most paper money belongs to the realm of modern history, where surviving documentation tends to overshadow the importance of the primary evidence presented by contemporary objects. The reality is that the dispersal and destruction of so many printers' and banks' archives is turning the surviving pieces of paper money into the most direct and informative evidence of their own production and issue. The case study chosen is a good example of this. The Hongkong Bank's archives are still largely intact (damaged only by the circumstances of war and revolution), thanks to the Bank's commitment to preserving its own history, and much of its public activity as a note issuer is recorded in British Government official reports and archives because of its role as the chief provider of Hong Kong's official money. However, the archives of the printers, Barclay & Fry, have been completely disbanded or destroyed. Thanks to the activities of one collector, some of this lost material can be reassembled, but it is a tiny proportion of the whole archive which must have once existed.

A typical example of this process of loss is the possible fate of the sample books of a certain Mr Eric Powell, who represented Barclay & Fry in the Far East. The contents of these books were offered for sale through Sotheby's London sale room on 1 October 1987. The books themselves were already taken apart and not offered for sale. The notes were divided up into lots, some apparently reflecting the grouping of the notes in the sample books, and sold to the highest bidders. The whole of the Hongkong Bank's note issue for Hong Kong from 1867 to 1899 was represented by forty-nine notes in the sample books. They were divided into twenty-five lots, with brief descriptions mentioning colours, denominations and dates; any manuscript annotations on the notes (mostly dates) were also mentioned. There was, however, only a single illustration of one side of just one of these notes. Fortunately, however, forty-seven of the forty-nine notes were purchased by one collector and I have been able to examine most of them as part of this research. Five of the forty-nine notes were $1 denominations and are therefore not covered by this paper. The remaining forty-four notes represent 25% of the surviving notes recorded in the course of this research. If they had been split up through the sale the evidence they provide would no longer be available. The same collector's interest in the history of Barclay & Fry has also preserved a few other important pieces of information concerning the 1865–98 notes of the Hongkong Bank, which have been included in this study.

The main results of my research are presented here in the form of tables out-lining the chronological progression of note production in a series of phases. Because of the different design adopted for the $5 denomination after phase III, the varieties of this denomination are listed in phases distinct from the other denominations, even though their production was parallel to that of the higher denominations.

The initial step in classification was to collect the details of as many notes as possible. When my work on the 1987 book was completed, the material from the Barclay & Fry sample books was not yet available to me, so this study represents a further refinement of the classification presented in 1987. I have also been able to spend more time since then looking at the process of plate change by examining at first hand the examples in William Barrett's collection, including the Eric Powell sample book specimens, and this has added further detail to the classification. Within the limits set out above, 161 notes have been recorded during this study. In addition to these I have included three contemporary forgeries and four notes printed for Hong Kong which the Bank overprinted for issue at other branches. There are also up to seven more notes listed by Lam which cannot be included because of the lack of reported information or their probable misidentification.

The limited number of the notes available highlights the nature of the problems involved in classifying them and studying the history of their production and issue. There were an estimated 1,000,000 notes of the range covered by this study issued in Hong Kong. I have been able to record only forty-nine issued notes (i.e. about 0.005%), and the random nature of their survival (there are no issued $500 notes recorded, for example) means that such a number can hardly be described as a representative sample.

The other 112 notes are far more useful for classification, because, as printer's specimens and proofs, their survival has been more intentional and systematic. An almost complete record of the plate-making and printing activities of the printer can be reconstructed from the specimens and proofs, but they lack the important additions of information available from issued examples. The process of issue required the printer to add various elements to each note by letterpress. In separate processes the printer would add the serial number, and after 1884 the signature of the Bank's Chief Manager, and from 1888 to 1893 the date of first issue. From 1893 (1891 for $5 notes) the date was added at an earlier stage as part of the main printing plate and so also appeared on specimen notes. At the place of issue each note had handwritten additions made. Initially these were the signatures of the Manager or Chief Manager and Accountant or Chief Accountant, and the first date of issue. These were gradually replaced by the printed additions listed above, but the (Chief) Accountant's signature continued to be added by hand to all notes, and the Chief Manager's signature was still required on $500 notes throughout the period in question. The handwritten signatures appearing were normally not those of the named officials, but of subordinates signing on their behalf.

The usefulness of the issued notes in classification is primarily based on the added information outlined above, but apart from the rarity of such notes there is another limitation to the role they can play. Because they have been in circulation, issued notes are often in deteriorated condition. The details added by hand might have faded and be illegible; the colours of the printer's ink can also fade, changing their intended colour; corners of the note can be torn off, and indeed in many cases were intentionally cut off on cancellation.

The additions on the issued notes, particularly serial numbers and dates, are vital for understanding the sequence of issue by the Bank, but such a limited random sample can go only a small way towards creating a full picture. However, this limitation is compensated for in the case of the Hongkong Bank by the survival in the Bank's archives of the issue record of the Bank's Hong Kong notes. This record takes the form of Bank Note Issue Registers, which list by serial number the notes issued by the Bank. Each opening of a register presents two pages with 250 notes listed on each page. At the head of each page are the dates of signing (nominally the date of first issue) and the date of actual issue from the Hong Kong Office. The notes were signed in batches of 500 (i.e. one opening of the register), with the samples of the two signatories at the head of each page. As each note was withdrawn from circulation and paid off by the Bank, the date of cancellation was entered into the register opposite the serial number. The registers show that fewer than 1% of the issued notes were not returned to the Bank for cancellation. It is interesting to note that thirty-four of the known surviving issued notes had been returned to the Bank for cancellation (mostly preserved for an unknown reason by the Bank from two batches cancelled in 1904 and 1911), leaving only fifteen of the recorded issued notes, twelve $5 and three $10, surviving from circulation. The registers show exactly how many notes the Bank put into circulation, but there is no indication of the varieties of notes being issued. It is therefore necessary to return to the relatively small number of recorded surviving issued notes and specimens in order to try to match the issue registers with the activities of the printer on behalf of the Bank.

The first step was to arrange the notes by denomination and then place them in sequence by date and serial number. The dates could appear in four different forms: added by hand to issued notes, printed on issued notes by letterpress, printed on the notes as part of the main printing plate, and written onto the edge of the note as a printer's annotation. Then each note was compared with the notes before and after it in the sequence in order to identify any observable changes in the details of the printing plate and the added elements.

This process of comparison showed that there were regular changes of details, but these were not accompanied by complete change of the rest of the design. For example, the change from phase I to phase II involved only the elements relating to the Bank's name. For all recorded examples this just meant changing the inscription in the central panel from 'THE HONGKONG & SHANGHAI COMPANY, LIMITED' to 'THE HONGKONG & SHANGHAI CORPORATION'. Altering the inscription also disturbed the background pattern for the central panel and so a new background had to be engraved. Instead of the original wave pattern, a zigzag pattern made up of staggered repetitions of the denomination in words was used. Examination of the notes showed that the remaining details were unchanged. This change could not have been achieved by re-engraving the steel printing plates already in use, because the design to be changed was cut into the surface of the steel plate. The only way it could have been done was for a positive impression of the plate to be made and the central panel erased, then this altered impression used to impress a new printing plate which could then be engraved with the new version of the central panel. This could be done using a process developed earlier in the nineteenth century by the American inventor Jacob Perkins. This process involved transferring the design from an engraved hardened steel printing plate by pressure onto a softened steel roller, then hardening the roller in order to transfer the original design onto a softened steel plate, which would be hardened before further use for printing or to retransfer the design to another roller in the same way. The design on the roller was raised above the surface and parts of it could therefore be erased to create a smooth level surface; once transferred back on to a flat plate this erased area could again be decorated with a new engraved design cut into its level surface, while the rest of the design remained unaltered.

The process was repeatedly used by the printers as progressive design changes were required by the Hongkong Bank. The nature of these changes provides evidence for the sequence of designs. General observation of the notes readily identifies major changes, such as in the colour of the inks used, in the name of the Bank, in the form of the overprint, and so on, but the examination of the minute details gives a clearer record of the printers' activities on the Bank's behalf. Once a general picture of these changes is obtained, then the specimen notes without dates or numbers and issued notes in damaged condition can easily be placed in the sequence.

The tables presented here show the results achieved by this examination. The phases reflect easily observable major changes, as indicated above, and the varieties within each phase represent the intentional changes resulting from the production of new printing plates or new added features such as printed signatures (the nature of the changes are indicated in the table). New plates and changes in added features were normally made in response to requests by the Bank, but in some cases new slightly modified plates were made when the previous plate had worn out (for example, see the varieties of $5 plates for phase III). The modifications were apparently necessary to rework worn areas of the design which did not transfer effectively in the plate to roller to plate process described above. During the period covered by this study only one completely new plate had to be made, for the $5 denomination in 1893 (used from phase IXc).

The tabulation of the material serves to allay one doubt which could be raised over the nature of the surviving printer's specimens from Eric Powell's sample books. It is a possibility that specimens could have been printed from stock plates all at one go to make up the sample books, but the exact coincidence of printing plates between hand-dated specimens and issued notes of the same date confirm that the specimens were printed at the time of issue and later collected for the sample books. This is also confirmed by the changing but consistent pattern of the use of the printer's perforated cancellation punch, normally applied once only until 1889 (twice on $500 specimens), four times from 1890, except three times in early 1893 and early 1897 and twice in 1898.

The survival of the notes from the sample book has consolidated the results of the process of classification, but the Issue Registers and printer's archive material are necessary to fill some gaps. For example, the Issue Registers confirm the delivery of phase I $10 notes to the Bank and their use at Fuzhou in 1867, even though no examples have been seen. The dating of phase IIIa notes to 1878, although they are known only from specimens, is based on the record of paper use at Barclay & Fry during 1877-9, surviving in William Barrett's collection (this document incidentally reveals the reason for the single cut end of the notes of this period, because twice as many notes were printed as pieces of paper used, suggesting that each piece of paper was cut in two). Another document in the same collection gives the date at which Barclay & Fry took over the business of the previous printer, Ashby. This document is a letter from the printer to the Bank concerning a note thought to be a forgery, but proving to be a genuine note with a printing error. The letter refers to the printing of the note (phase IIa $50 note issued in 1870) in 1867, its delivery in 1867 as part of a batch of 5,000 notes, and the acquisition of Ashby in 1870. The note has survived with the letter, and is the second oldest surviving issued note of the Bank. The third oldest issued note survived for the same reason; it was in the private collection of the Solicitor General of Hong Kong, identified as a forgery because of its lack of the usual watermark. Its authenticity is now confirmed by comparison of the printing plate with surviving specimens, and the lack of watermark was admitted as an observed error by the paper supplier during the first decade of note production in the letter in William Barrett's collection.

The creation of these tables makes it possible to document the record of the Bank's note production, and to attribute precisely all the undated specimens which have survived. This information also brings out further insights into note production and use. The recorded serial numbers and the Issue Registers help to give an over-view of the rate of note issue, which can be compared with reports of the volume of notes in circulation contained in the official government records. The Hong Kong Government Annual Blue Books report annual figures for the total value of the Bank's notes in circulation, rising from about $800,000 by the end of 1865 to about $1,700,000 by the end of 1880, about $3,400,000 by the end of 1890 and about $7,500,000 at the end of 1899. In order to achieve this level of usage, production had to grow at an increasingly higher rate. By 1890 the Bank had issued about $10,000,000 worth of notes (i.e. about three times the amount in use), while by 1899 it had issued $56,000,000 (i.e. about seven-and-a-half times the amount in use. The rapid increase in note use during the last decade of the century was achieved by a huge increase in the issue of notes at a rate far in excess of the number staying in circulation. More detailed study of the Issue Registers would further refine the information derived in this way on the apparatus of the growth of money supply in late nineteenth-century Hong Kong.

The study of the serial numbers and dates of printing in relation to the process of plate change also yields interesting results. For example, the growth in the demand for the Bank's notes is reflected in an acceleration in the rate of plate replacement. Thus in the period 1865–75 only two front plates were used to print $5 notes, for 1876–85 four plates, and for 1886–95 seven plates. In the case of the $5 denomination it is also possible to compare the number of plates against the number of notes and show that each plate was used to print about 40,000–50,000 notes. Similar comparisons for the other denominations show 25,000 for $10, 13,750 for $25, 11,000 for $50, 5,000 for $100, 3,000 for $500. This shows that the replacement of plates for the $5 denomination could occasionally be caused by the printing plate being worn out, but that plate replacement for higher denominations was more dependent upon changes requested by the Bank, because production levels did not exhaust the potential of the printing plates. Research on the contemporary $1 notes supports this. The record of paper use at Barclay & Fry during 1877–9 mentioned above states that 300,000 $1 notes were printed during the same period as 50,000 $5 notes were produced. The printer was using six separate printing plates for $1 notes at the same time as printing plate 1c (phase IIIa) was being used to print the 50,000 $5 notes. Much is learnt from this exercise about the productivity of Barclay & Fry during this period.

There are many more pieces of information to be extracted as a result of this study. It provides a framework for attributing newly discovered notes, and for continuing the process of exploring the history of banknote printing, production and use in the nineteenth century. My intention here was not to answer all the questions, but to show how much information can be gained from such a small sample, and how valuable archival material can be in understanding the history of paper money. During the nineteenth century British printers and the commercial banks of the British world who were their customers played a key role in the establishment of paper money as a commonplace element of social intercourse world wide. The surviving examples of the notes they printed and issued merit close attention as important historical evidence for this key element in the development of modern money.

Acknowledgements

I would like to thank William Barrett both for making available to me much of the material on which this study has been based, and especially for his generous contributions of encouragement, insights, advice and resources. Thanks are also due to the following who have freely made material available: Stuart Muirhead, former archivist of the Hongkong Bank Group, my mentor during the production of *Money in the Bank*; the present archivist Margaret Lee; Edwin Green and Sarah Kinsey of the Midland Bank Archives; Mark Blackburn of the Fitzwilliam Museum, Cambridge; and James Morton of Sotheby, London. I have also relied heavily on the support and encouragement of my colleagues Virginia Hewitt, Helen Wang, Andrew Burnett, Annette Calton and Tony Hughes; I thank them.

Bibliography

COLLIS, M., *Wayfoong, The Hongkong and Shanghai Banking Corporation*, rev. edn, London 1978.

CRIBB, J., *Money in the Bank: An Illustrated Introduction to the Money Collection of The Hongkong and Shanghai Banking Corporation*, London 1987.

KING, F.H.H., *The History of The Hongkong and Shanghai Banking Corporation*, vol. 1, *The Hongkong Bank in Late Imperial China 1864–1902*, Cambridge 1987.

LAM, R., *Currency of Hong Kong*, Hong Kong 1983; rev. edn, 1988.

MAO, K.O., *History of Chinese Paper Currency*, vol. II, *Occidental Banks in China*, Hong Kong 1977.

PICK, A., *Standard Catalog of World Paper Money*, 5th edn, Iola, Wisconsin 1986; 6th edn, 1990.

SEAR, J., 'Variety in the note issues of The Hongkong and Shanghai Banking Corporation 1865–1891', in F.H.H. King (ed.), *Eastern Banking: Essays on the History of The Hongkong and Shanghai Banking Corporation*, London 1983, pp. 139–49.

SMITH, W.D., and MALTRAVERS, B., *Chinese Banknotes*, Menlo Park, California 1970.

Tables

Specimens are sample notes made by the printers to demonstrate their products.

Words in inverted commas are manuscript notes on specimens.

Words in italics are printed on the notes.

1a, 1b, 1c, etc., are my numbers for the main printing plates of the obverse designs recorded in this study.

Phase I   Ashby black with blue Company notes (fig. 1)

Bank title: *The Hongkong & Shanghai Banking Company, Limited*
Printer's mark: *Engraved on Steel by Ashby & Co. London* (with *E.C.* added on $10 and $50)
Central panel: Wave pattern
Colours: Fronts: all denominations are black, with blue overprint; backs: each denomination a different colour ($5 green; $10 red; $25 orange; $50 black; $100 red; $500 black); numbers are added by letterpress in black

Phase	Date	$5	$10	$25	$50	$100	$500
I	1865	**1a** Specimen×1	**1a** not seen	**1a** Specimen×1 (front only)	**1a** Forgery×1	**1a** Forgery×1	**1a** Specimen×1 (back only)
	1866			**1a** [Phase I notes issued at Yokohama]			
	1867		**1a** [Phase I notes issued at Fuzhou]				

The Issue Registers (in the Archives of HSBC Holdings plc) show that the first notes printed for the Bank were delivered from June 1865 until January 1866, dispatched by the printer Ashby & Co. in small batches. They were issued until the phase II notes arrived.

Phase II Ashby black with blue Corporation notes (fig. 2)

(from 1870 signed 'Ashby', but printed by Barclay & Fry)

As phase I, with the following exceptions:
Bank title: *The Hongkong & Shanghai Banking Corporation*
Central panel: Zigzag pattern composed of staggered lines with denomination in words
Variations: a with officers' titles *Accountant* and *Manager* **b** with officers' titles *Accountant* and *Chief Manager*
The Barclay & Fry Sample Books of Mr Eric Powell contained:
Sample set for phase IIa containing all denominations except $500 (all perforated CANCELLED ×1)
Hongkong and Shanghai Bank Money Collection contains:
Sample set for phase IIa containing all denominations except $100 (all with oval stamp JUL 16 1877 CANCELLED)
Sample set for phase IIb containing all denominations except $5 (all with oval stamp SEP 4 1877 CANCELLED)

Phase	Date	$5	$10	$25	$50	$100	$500
IIa	1867	**1b** Specimen×3 +Issued×1	**1b** Specimen×2	**1b** Specimen×2	**1b** Specimen×2	**1b** Specimen×2 +Proof×1	**1b** Specimen×1
	1868						
	1869						
	1870				**1b** Issued×1		
	1871						
IIb	1872		**1c** Specimen×1	**1c** Specimen×1	**1c** Specimen×1	**1c** Specimen×1	**1c** Specimen×1
	1873						
	1874						
	1875						
	1876						
	1877	**1c** Issued×1					

IIa The change from Company to Corporation took place in December 1866, but the change was already anticipated in the instructions to the printers, who, according to a letter in Barrett's collection, sent proofs of phase IIa notes to the Bank from April 1866. An issued example shows that $5 notes were available for issue on 1 January 1867. The letter in Barrett's collection mentions the arrival of $50 notes later the same month.
IIb The Manager became Chief Manager in 1868, but phase IIb notes reflecting this change of title were not available until 1872, when $1 notes showing this characteristic were issued. It is probable that the printer received the instruction to print these well before 1872, because the new printing plates for the $1 notes had the name of Ashby engraved on them while according to Barrett's letter Barclay & Fry had bought out Ashby in April 1870.

Phase III 'Ashby' coloured notes (fig. 3)
(printed by Barclay & Fry)

As Phase IIb, with the following exceptions:
Printed signature of Chief Manager introduced on last variety of this phase
Colours: Fronts: each denomination a different colour ($5 green; $10 blue; $25 brown; $50 purple; $100 red; $500 red); with contrasting overprints (red for $5, $10, $25, $50, blue for $100 and green for $500); backs: all denominations red; printed signatures added in black on some notes
Variations: a as notes of phase IIb **b** new printing plate (arms and central panel changed) **c** new printing plate (arms, border and corner motifs changed) **d** new printing plate (lines for signatures removed, central panel changed); Chief Manager's printed signature *T. Jackson*
The Barclay & Fry Sample Books of Mr Eric Powell contained:
Sample set for phase IIIa containing all denominations except $100 (all perforated CANCELLED ×1, except $500×2)

Phase	Date	$5	$10	$25	$50	$100	$500
IIIa	1878	**1c** Specimen×2	**1c** Specimen×1	**1c** Specimen×2	**1d** Specimen×2	**1c** not seen	**1c** Specimen×2
	1879						
	1880						
IIIb	1881	**1d** Issued×2					
	1882	**1d** Issued×3					
IIIc	1883	**1e** Issued×1					
IIId	1884	**1f** Issued×4		**1c** [Phase IIIa notes issued at Fuzhou]	**1d** Issued×1 [Phase IIIa notes issued at Fuzhou]		

IIIa–c   This phase merely involved changes in colour, not design (except that a new plate was made for the $50 denomination). The phase is dated by the printer's record of paper use during 1877–9 in Barrett's collection. Variations b and c represent the replacement of worn-out $5 printing plates.

IIId   The first use of a printed Chief Manager's signature, a feature already used on $1 notes from 1872.

Phase IV   Barclay & Fry coloured notes

As phase III, with the following exceptions:
No $5 notes (see phase VIa for contemporary issues of this denomination)
No printed signatures
Printer's mark: *Engraved on Steel by Barclay & Fry, London*
Officers' titles: *Chief Accountant* and *Chief Manager*
The Barclay & Fry Sample Books of Mr Eric Powell contained:
Sample set for phase IVa containing $10, $50, $100 and $500 (all dated '1884' and perforated CANCELLED×1 except $500×2)

Phase	Date	$5	$10	$25	$50	$100	$500
IV	1884		**1d** Specimen×1	**1d** Not seen	**1e** Specimen×1	**1d** Specimen×1	**1d** Specimen×1
	1885						
	1886	see VIa					
	1887						
	1888		**1d** Issued×2			**1d** Issued×1	
	1889			**1d** Issued×1			

The name of the printer is changed to Barclay & Fry, who had been printing the notes since April 1870. Otherwise the notes are the same as those printed for phase III. The phase is dated from manuscript dates on specimens.

Phase V   Barclay & Fry 'Wayfoong' $10–$500 notes (fig. 4)

As phase IV, with the following exceptions:

No $5 notes (see phases VIb–c and VII for contemporary issues of this denomination); $25 denomination abandoned because of forgeries

Changes in Chinese inscriptions

Denomination overprint in new form (cartouche)

Printed signatures introduced for Chief Manager (used on $5 since phase IIId)

Colour: Dates and printed signatures added by letterpress [lp] in black

Variations: a Chinese character in Bank's name changed (*li* becomes *feng*); Chief Manager's printed signature *T. Jackson* **b** Chinese character meaning dollar (*yuan*) with changed form; Chief Manager's printed signature *G.E. Noble*

The Barclay & Fry Sample Books of Mr Eric Powell contained:

Sample set for phase Va containing $50, $100 and $500 (all dated '1888' and perforated CANCELLED×1, except $500×2)

Sample set for phase Vb containing $10 and $100 (all dated '1889' and perforated CANCELLED×3, except $10×1), together with a $5 of phase VIIa

Phase	Date	$5	$10		$50	$100	$500
Va	1888	see VIb–c			**1f** Specimen×2	**1e** Specimen×2 +Issued×1	**1e** Specimen×2
Vb	1889	see VIIa	**1e** Specimen×2		**1g** Specimen×1	**1f** Specimen×2	
	1890		**1e** Issued×4 1.3.90[lp]		**1g** Issued×1 2.1.90[lp]	**1f** Issued×1 2.1.90[lp]	

A new design was introduced, with a new style of overprint and the Chinese name of the Bank changed from Waylee (*Huili*=remittance) to Wayfoong (*Huifeng*=abundance of remittances). This name had been in use on the Bank's Shanghai notes since 1865. The new overprint was in the form of a cartouche containing the denomination, a feature already used on Shanghai notes since 1885, and Hiogo-Kobe and Singapore notes since 1886.

Printed Chief Manager's signatures became standard from this issue (except on subsequent $500 notes). The varieties are distinguished by different signatures and dated by manuscript dates on specimens. Letterpress dates were introduced in phase Vb.

Phase VI   Barclay & Fry two-colour $5 notes (fig. 5)

As phase V, with the following exceptions:
$5 notes only (see phases IV and Va for contemporary issues of other denominations)
Central panel: The denomination is engraved in voided capitals
Colours: The overprint is yellow and does not indicate denomination, but fills the voided letters and the field of the note's main design
Variations: a without printed signature (proof dated '1886' by hand) **b** Chief Manager's printed signature *T. Jackson*

Phase	Date	$5	$10		$50	$100	$500
VIa	1886	**1g** Proof×2	see IVa		see IVa	see IVa	see IVa
	1887						
VIb	1888	**1h** Specimen×1 +Colour trial ×6 **1i** Issued×1 31.12.88[lp]	see Va		see Va	see Va	see Va

This is the first use of full two-colour notes by the Bank. At first used only for $5 notes, this new design was extended to higher denominations from 1890 (phase VIII) and to Shanghai notes from 1889.

From this phase all $5 notes also have their denomination engraved in large voided capital letters across the central panel, copying a design used on the Bank's Penang notes from 1885 (the innovation of a different printer).

Variations are distinguished by signature on VIb and dated by an issued note and the manuscript date on a specimen.

Phase VII   Barclay & Fry two-colour 'Wayfoong' $5 notes (fig. 6)

As phase VI, with the following exceptions:

$5 notes only (see phases Vb and VIIIa for contemporary issues of other denominations)

Changes in Chinese inscription: character in Bank's name changed (*li* becomes *feng*); character meaning dollar (*yuan*) with changed form

Variations: a new zigzag pattern on central panel; Chief Manager's signature *GE Noble* **b** without printed signature **c** _____ 18____ for date recut; Chief Manager's signature *F. de Bovis*

The Barclay & Fry Sample Books of Mr Eric Powell contained:

Samples for $5 notes of phases VIIa (dated '1889' and perforated CANCELLED×1), VIIb (dated '1890' and perforated CANCELLED×1), and VIIc (dated 'Jany 1893' and perforated CANCELLED×3)

Phase	Date	$5	$10		$50	$100	$500
VIIa	1889	**1j** Specimen×2 +Issued×1 1.12.89[lp]	see Vb		see Vb	see Vb	see Vb
	1890	**1j** Issued×1 2.1.90[lp]					
VIIb		**1j** Specimen×1	see VIIIa			see VIIIa	see VIIIa
	1891	see IXa					
	1892						
VIIc	1893	**1l** Specimen×2 +Issued×2 4.1.93[lp]	seeVIIIb		see VIIIb		

This phase saw the extension of the new Chinese name (see phase V) to the $5 denomination. Varieties are distinguished by changing printed signatures and dated by both issued notes and manuscript dates on specimens. The omission of the signature on phase VIIb was the consequence of a period of indecision by the Bank over who to appoint as its next Chief Manager (Thomas Jackson, a former Chief Manager, served as a stopgap during 1890).

Phase VIII   Barclay & Fry two-colour $10 – $500 notes (fig. 7)

As phase V, with the following exceptions:
No $5 notes (see phases VIIb–c and IXa for contemporary issues of this denomination)
The overprint is no longer the denomination, but fills the field of the main design
Colours (phases VIII and X): Each denomination has a different colour for the main plate and a contrasting colour for the filler overprint ($10 blue with red overprint; $50 purple with orange overprint; $100 red with blue overprint; $500 red with green overprint (these denominations now match the colour scheme of the $5 green with yellow overprint))
Variations: a without printed signature **b** Chief Manager's printed signature *F. de Bovis*
The Barclay & Fry Sample Books of Mr Eric Powell contained:
Sample set for phase VIIIa containing $10, $100 and $500 (all dated '1890' and perforated CANCELLED×4, except $100×3), together with a $5 of phase VIIb
Sample for $10 of phase VIIIb (dated 'Jany 1893' and perforated CANCELLED×3)

Phase	Date	$5	$10		$50	$100	$500
VIIIa	1890	see VIIb	**1e** Specimen×2 +Issued×1 15.12.90[lp]			**1f** Specimen×2	**1e** Specimen×2
	1891	see IXa					
	1892						
VIIIb	1893	see VIIc	**1e** Specimen×1		**1h** Specimen×1 +Proof×1		

The full two-colour design, introduced for $5 notes in phase VI, was applied to higher denominations.

Varieties were distinguished in the same way as on the notes of phase VII and dated by manuscript dates on specimens.

Phase IX   Barclay & Fry printed date $5 notes (fig. 8)

As phase VII, with the following exceptions:
$5 notes only (see phases VIII and X for contemporary issues of other denominations)
Dates printed as part of the main design, engraved on the main plate
Variations: a dated *2nd January 1891*; without printed signature **b** dated *1st April 1893*; Chief Manager's printed signature *F. de Bovis* **c** new version of main design; dated *1st September 1893*; Chief Manager's printed signature *T. Jackson* **d** dated *1st March 1896* **e** dated *1st March 1897* **f** dated *1st September 1897* **g** dated *1st March 1898*
The Barclay & Fry Sample Books of Mr Eric Powell contained:
Samples of $5 notes for phase IXa, b and f (perforated CANCELLED ×4)
Samples of $5 notes for phase IXd, e and g in sets with phase X notes (see below)

Phase X   Barclay & Fry printed date $10 – $500 notes (fig. 9)

As phase VIII, with the following exceptions:

No $5 notes (see phase IX for contemporary issues of this denomination)

Dates printed as part of the main design, engraved on the main plate

$500 retains earlier version of Chinese character for dollar (*yuan*) and lacks printed signature

Variations: a dated *1st April 1893*; Chief Manager's printed signature *F. de Bovis* **b** dated *1st September 1893*; Chief Manager's printed signature *T. Jackson* **c** dated *1st January 1895* **d** dated *1st March 1896* **e** dated *1st March 1897* **f** dated *1st September 1897* **g** dated *1st March 1898*

The Barclay & Fry Sample Books of Mr Eric Powell contained:

Samples of $10 notes for phase Xa (perforated CANCELLED×3) and f (perforated CANCELLED×4)

Sample of $100 note for phase Xb (perforated CANCELLED×4)

Sample of $500 note for phase Xc (perforated CANCELLED×4)

Sample set for phases IXd and Xd containing $5, $10, $100 and $500 (perforated CANCELLED×4)

Sample set for phases IXe and Xe containing $5, $10, $100 and $500 (perforated CANCELLED×3)

Sample set for phases IXg and Xg containing $5, $10 and $50 (perforated CANCELLED×2)

Phase	Date	$5	$10		$50	$100	$500
IXa	1891	1k Specimen×1 +Issued×1					
	1892						
IXb/Xa	1893	1m Specimen×2 +Issued×1	1f Specimen×2 +Issued×3				
IXc/Xb		2a Issued×2				1g Specimen×2 +Issued×2	
	1894						
– /Xc	1895					1h Specimen×1 +Issued×1	1f Specimen×1
IXd/Xd	1896	2b Specimen×1	1g Specimen×2 +Issued×1			1i Specimen×3	1g Specimen×3
IXe/Xe	1897	2c Specimen×2	1h Specimen×3		1i Specimen×1 +Issued×1	1j Specimen×2	1h Specimen×2
IXf/Xf		2d Specimen×2 +Issued×1	1i Specimen×4 +Issued×1				
IXg/Xg	1898	2e Specimen×3 +Issued×2	1j Specimen×3 +Issued×2 +Forgery×1		1j Specimen×4 +Issued×1		

The innovations of phases VII and VIII were continued, but with printed dates added as part of the main design. Varieties are distinguished and dated by their changing dates. Increasing volume of issue during the last decade of the century enabled the Bank to predict more accurately when the next issue was needed and the quantity of notes of each denomination needed for it, so the dating of notes at printing became more convenient. These phases represent the end of Barclay & Fry's work for the Bank's Hong Kong Office. A specimen $100 note for Hong Kong printed in 1888 by Bradbury & Wilkinson, using new plate-making technology, suggests that the Bank had already been considering terminating the contract for several years.

1 Phase I, $5 specimen note (1865), plate 1a, black with blue overprint.

2 Phase IIa, $50 issued note dated 1 June 1870, plate 1b, black with blue overprint.

3 Phase IIIa, $25 specimen note (1878), plate 1c, brown with red overprint.

4 Phase Vb, $10 issued note dated 1 March 1890, plate 1e, blue with red overprint.

5 Phase VIa, $5 proof annotated 'Nov 1886', plate 1g, green with yellow overprint.

6 Phase VIIa, $5 specimen note, annotated '1889', plate 1j, green with yellow overprint.

7 Phase VIIIa, $100 specimen note, annotated '1890', plate 1f, red with blue overprint.

8 Phase IXc, $5 issued note dated 1 September 1893, plate 2a, green with yellow overprint.

9 Phase X, $500 specimen note dated 1 March 1897, plate 1h, red with green overprint.

PART TWO

MAKING PAPER MONEY – DESIGN AND SYMBOLISM

7

Compound-plate printing and the nineteenth-century banknote

Maureen Greenland

Research into the history and technology of a printing process inevitably involves a study of the printed items themselves. The subject of this paper is part of a wider investigation into compound-plate printing, a security printing method which originated from the need to protect revenue stamps. The attempt to unearth information has led into the realms of matchboxes and blacking labels, advertisements for lotteries, and the beautiful tickets for seats at the coronation of George IV. Banknotes also play a small but significant part in the history of this versatile printing process, which was used for note designs and for banknote duty stamps.

When Sir William Congreve patented the method in 1821 (patent no. 4521), the first compound-plate printing press was already at work printing banknotes at Somerset House. Congreve's invention was a printing plate constructed in two interlocking parts, which would print simultaneously in two colours. At the time, colour printing was in its infancy: black-on-white prints from copper plates were the norm. The visual impact of the bicoloured, relief-printed impressions, taken from the intricately engraved compound plates, can be appreciated in the printer Charles Whiting's own advertisement (col. plate 5). The engraver was Whiting's partner, Robert Branston, who used a 'rose engine' geometric lathe to create networks of fine patterns cut into a bronze die. When the ink was applied to the surface of the die, the engraved lines remained uncoloured, appearing white on the final product. Because the protrusions on the lower plate exactly fitted the filigree of the upper section, no gaps or overlaps of colour could occur (col. plate 6).

The ingenious rose engine was built by Bryan Donkin, a brilliant engineer best known for his development of the Fourdrinier paper-making machine. Donkin also constructed the unusual printing press on which the two sections of the printing die were separated and inked in two different colours, before being brought together to form the two-colour design that was transferred to the paper. The result was an elaborate print which was difficult to reproduce without the specialised equipment.

Banknote forgery was rife at the beginning of the nineteenth century. Death was the ultimate penalty for counterfeiting, and the possessor of a forged note faced a fourteen-year prison sentence, yet hundreds of impecunious engravers were willing to take the risk. Many members of the public were illiterate and, like the public today, not sufficiently visually aware to be able to discriminate between genuine and false notes; even government inspectors had difficulty in identifying the counterfeits, a point sharply made in several satirical cartoons of the time.

In 1818 both the government and the Society of Arts instituted enquiries inviting suggestions for solutions to the problem. Hundreds of anti-forgery ideas poured in. All were considered – special papers, engraving by machine, the use of steel printing plates, secret marks and tiny printing types – but the outcome was indecisive and the Bank of England retained its traditional black-and-white note.

A strong contender in the security printing business was Jacob Perkins, an American inventor who came to England in 1819 to promote his system of sidero-graphy, a method of transferring engraved designs on to steel printing plates. He and Congreve both offered their ideas to the Bank and became bitter rivals, issuing threats and challenges in private letters and public magazines, in a feud that lasted for years. Both were turned down by the Bank of England, but found custom among the many private banks operating in Britain at this time.

At least ten of the provincial banks were persuaded that compound-plate printing would offer protection to their notes, and adopted designs probably produced by Whiting and Branston, using Congreve's invention. The first to take advantage of the two-colour method appear to have been banks in Deal (col. plate 7) and Plymouth in the early 1820s; others soon followed suit and later two banks, the Bank of Sheffield and Rotherham and the Bank of Ireland, commissioned a variation of the method in which part of the lettering was printed in red and black against a white background. Several foreign banks, including some in Boulogne, Cape of Good Hope and Hindustan, also had their notes designed and printed by Whiting. By the end of the 1830s most of the banks had abandoned the bicoloured notes, but the Deal Bank kept their attractive design at least until 1870, and Stuckey's Somersetshire Bank continued to use their striking red-and-black reverse design until 1909 (col. plate 8). Used in this way, it seems that compound-plate printing was successful as a deterrent to forgers: not a single forgery of these notes has come to light.

Notes issued by country banks were subject to taxation, with a 5d duty levied on a £1 note and 1s 3d on £5. Until 1821 the stamp that signified the payment of the duty was embossed on to the note, but being colourless the mark soon became indistinct; it was also subject to abuse by forgers. The government therefore approved a new compound-plate printed duty stamp to replace the embossed one, and from 1821 a large black-and-red design was printed on the reverse of the provincial banknotes (col. plate 9).

A confusing situation arose over the next four years, when six different but similar stamps were issued in succession for £1 notes and three for £5 notes (col. plate 10). Old notes were not necessarily withdrawn when a new design was introduced, with the result that at least three different stamps were always in circulation on the notes; in 1825 there were no less than six throughout the country. Each design, though beautifully executed, must have appeared to the man in the street as a jumble of red and black, and he had little chance of spotting a forgery. Public confusion worked to the forger's advantage and there were many attempts at counterfeiting, ranging from poor efforts to excellent copies (col. plate 11). A new series of designs, introduced in 1825, were of a similar, circular format with an embossed centre featuring St George and the Dragon for the 5d duty, or the king's head on the 1s 3d duty stamp (col. plate 12). Even the most accomplished forgers made mistakes, however: a crooked Rochdale engraver made an excellent facsimile of a £5 note with the wrong central motif (col. plate 13). The engraver of one of the many fake Dundee notes, for the Dundee Commercial Bank, made an almost perfect copy, but failed to notice that the leaves on one of the wreaths in his design were pointing in the wrong direction.

Complaints from bankers brought matters to a head, and in 1826 a government inquiry was held into Stamp Office practice. The ensuing report concluded that forgeries had increased since the introduction of compound-plate printing. Furthermore, setting up and running the machine had proved more costly than anticipated. Among the witnesses were printers who gave evidence that their notes took as long as ten days to return from the stamping office whereas the old stamp had required only one day. It was recommended, therefore, that the use of the stamp should cease to be mandatory after 1828, but in practice stamps continued to be issued until 1845 and some bankers elected to endow their notes with this stamp of authority until long after its official demise.

Compound-plate printing may not have been successful for banknote duty stamps, but there were few problems in other official spheres. The duty on paper was recognised for nearly forty years by a large compound-plate printed label; the only known forgeries were perpetrated by tampering with the handwritten additions. The medicine duty label, obligatory for patent medicine packets from 1823 until 1941, was rarely forged in this country, although numerous counterfeits were made to complement the forged labels for fake 'English' products in America. The Bryan Donkin Company continued to manufacture compound-plate printing plates for Indian revenue stamps until the early 1850s. Although this inventive method of colour printing did not fulfil its potential as a security measure against the forgery of the banknote duty stamps, it nevertheless achieved success in several other areas of official and commercial printing, including the protection of provincial banknotes when used as an integral part of the note design.

Acknowledgements

Illustrations are reproduced by kind permission of the Royal Philatelic Society (col. plate 6), the Trustees of the British Museum (col. plates 7, 8, 9, 11, 13), and the British Library (col. plates 10 and 12).

Bibliography

GREENLAND, M.L. AND DAY, R.E., *Compound-plate Printing*, The Foundation for Ephemera Studies, London 1990.

HEWITT, V.H. AND KEYWORTH, J., *As Good as Gold: 300 Years of British Bank Note Design*, London 1987.

MACKENZIE, A.D., *The Bank of England Note*, Cambridge 1953.

TWYMAN, M., *Printing 1770–1870*, London 1970.

Report of the Society for the Encouragement of Arts, Manufacturers, and Commerce, relative to the Mode of preventing the Forgery of Bank Notes, London 1819.

Report of the Commission of Inquiry into the Mode of Preventing Forgery in Bank Notes, London 1819.

Report of the Commission of Inquiry into the Collection and Management of the Revenue, London 1826.

Archives of the Bryan Donkin Company, Chesterfield and the Royal Philatelic Society, London.

The author is currently working on a Ph.D. thesis on the subject of compound-plate printing.

8

Printing Spanish banknotes in England, 1850–1938

Teresa Tortella

For almost a hundred years, from the middle of the nineteenth century until the 1930s, most Spanish banknotes were printed in England. In such a long period there are many small details and nuances to be studied, but in this paper I would just like to look briefly at why foreign printers were used, which firms were chosen, and what influence they had on the designs of the Spanish notes.[1] But I would like to begin by saying a little about the first notes issued in Spain.

The earliest Spanish notes recorded are those of the Banco de San Carlos, the first predecessor of the Banco de España (Bank of Spain), which were issued in Madrid in March 1783.[2] They were not widely accepted by the general public, and after the discovery of counterfeiting they were withdrawn from circulation. In 1829 the Banco de San Fernando was founded as the new official bank from the remains of the liquidated Banco de San Carlos, and given a monopoly for the issue of banknotes in Madrid. Another bank was created in Madrid in 1844, the Banco de Isabel II, which became the main competitor of the Banco de San Fernando. It was a private bank founded by a new generation of Spanish bankers and merchants whose main objectives were to finance industry and trade, especially railway companies. This bank was authorised to engage in all ordinary banking operations including the issue of banknotes. After almost four years of increasing confrontation the two banks merged in 1847 under the name of Nuevo Banco Español de San Fernando. Some years later in 1856, under a banking law approved by the Spanish Parliament, the bank received the name by which it is known today, the Banco de España or Bank of Spain. Finally in 1874 a decree by the Minister of Finance granted the Bank the monopoly of the right to issue banknotes throughout the country.

From 1783 to 1848 there were eleven different note issues. All of them were printed in Madrid by different printing companies. Each and every one of these issues, in their individual series or denominations, was counterfeited and this was the deciding factor which persuaded the Board of Directors of the Banco de San Fernando to commission an English printer in 1849.

The archives of the Bank of Spain contain a surprising amount of material on at least three English printing firms who worked for a considerable time first for the Banco de San Fernando, later for the Bank of Spain.[3] T.H. Saunders[4] was the first of these firms, commissioned to print the notes between 1850 and 1866, and in 1875. Then for a period of more than thirty years Spanish notes were printed on the premises of the Bank of Spain, except for two issues produced by the American Bank Note Company in 1876 and 1884. In the early years of the twentieth century, the Bank again asked an English printer to work for them. On this occasion they chose Bradbury, Wilkinson & Co., who printed Spanish notes from the beginning of the twentieth century until the end of the Spanish Civil War in 1939. At the end of the Second Republic and during the Civil War, another major English printer, Thomas De La Rue, worked simultaneously for the Bank on different note issues. Finally I must mention Waterlow & Sons, a third important English engraving and printing company that tried to work for the Bank of Spain when the contracts with the other two were cancelled after the Spanish Civil War. Their offer to print the notes was refused, but we know from the records that they were given the job of printing treasury bonds.

T.H. Saunders worked continuously for the Bank of Spain over a period of sixteen years and produced five issues (in 1850, 1852, 1856, 1862 and 1866), each with different denominations. Times were changing: as paper money was starting to be more widely used by the public, the Bank gradually needed to increase the number of banknotes in circulation and thus rely on the manufacturers for frequent new issues. Another important reason for the frequency of new issues was that in only twelve years, from 1862 to 1874, the Spanish monetary unit changed first from reales to escudos and then to pesetas.

T.H. Saunders' banknotes (figs 1–3) were quite different from those printed by the Spanish establishments that I have already mentioned. The main objective of the Bank was to prevent counterfeiting, and the more advanced printing techniques that were being used in England proved to be very effective for this purpose. Even though some of the new banknotes were also forged, it was on a small scale and they were easy to detect and distinguish from the genuine.

From the correspondence between T.H. Saunders and the Bank we know that his firm was responsible for the whole process of manufacturing the notes. First, he made proposals and set conditions that were generally accepted by the Bank.[5] Then the complete process was undertaken by Saunders, with the exception of the 1856 issue, when the Board of Directors of the Bank decided that the drawings and engraving of the plates should be undertaken by another firm in Britain, Perkins, Bacon & Co. (fig. 2). Normally, however, Saunders made the moulds and the watermarked paper and arranged for the engraving and production of the plates, printing and binding; although this is not clearly explained in his letters, it appears that he made the paper and subcontracted the rest of the process, all of which took place in England.[6] This is probably why these banknotes look so different from their Spanish predecessors – they have a strong British influence in their design, resembling notes printed for banks in England, Scotland and Ireland by other British firms using machine-engraving and small hand-engravings of allegorical figures. This is particularly evident on the note designed and engraved by Perkins Bacon, who produced notes for many banks in Britain and overseas. On Saunders' early issues for the Banco de San Fernando, many innovations were introduced: the whole engraving was made in black ink on coloured paper; the note had two borders, on the right and left sides with a design showing the name of the Bank; the serial number was printed and appeared twice, on the left and right sides of the note; and, although the denomination and date had been printed on earlier notes, they too now appeared twice. Saunders' first design (fig. 1) also included a decorative vignette with allegorical figures of Mercury and Glory supporting the Bank's emblem, two clasped hands with the motto '*fides publica*'. All the notes produced by Saunders were printed on the obverse only.

Later, important new technical elements considered as the best guarantee against forgery were adopted, such as the use of more vignettes of much more elaborate character, and of microscopic writing in the background of the note. As a general consideration we can say that in the last issues he produced for the Bank, Saunders used three separate printing processes: lithography for the background design; letterpress for the borders, margins and counterfoils; and intaglio for the rest of the design (fig. 3). Indeed, the Spanish Government chose the 1856 and 1862 issues as examples of fine artistic quality for the World Exhibition in Paris in 1867.

From the mid-1870s to the early 1900s, the Bank's notes were again printed in Spain, as the administration of the Bank decided it would be more convenient and would save time. However, they still had to face the same two problems, the increasing need for banknotes on the one hand and, on the other, the continual danger of counterfeiting. Thus in 1906 the Bank turned once again to an English printer, with the Board of Directors asking Bradbury, Wilkinson & Co. to produce a new issue with urgency (col. plates 14, 15). For the next twenty-eight years, this company was the only one who worked for the Bank. They were responsible for at least ten issues which coincided with the expansion of the circulation of banknotes. Again it is clear that the English techniques proved to be very much more advanced than those available in Spain, and again the Spanish banknotes seem to have a strong British influence in their style and design. However, during this period, the administration of the Bank gradually imposed their own conditions and character. First, the shield of Spain appeared on the reverse of the note (col. plate 15); later, portraits of Spanish monarchs or famous figures appeared on the obverse, with views of buildings or historical scenes on the reverse (col. plates 16, 17). The result was a series of notes in the recognisable style of Bradbury Wilkinson, but illustrating subjects which belonged specifically to Spain. For some Spanish specialists this is considered as the 'Golden Age' of Spanish banknotes.

The political change that took place in Spain in 1931 with the establishment of the Second Republic resulted in the decision to commission a third British printer, Thomas De La Rue. The political circumstances had an interesting effect on the banknotes, for the Republican government decided to change the design content of earlier notes in circulation under the Monarchy. A decree issued by the First Provisional Government of the Republic stated that new notes should show allegorical figures with representations of Republican symbols. At the same time, the new Board of Directors of the Bank was trying to find another note supplier since Bradbury Wilkinson had lost five 25 peseta notes from the issue of 25 April 1931, before they had officially been put into circulation. In addition, the estimates for new note issues submitted by De La Rue were clearly more economical than those from Bradbury Wilkinson. These last two practical points were the main factors in the Bank's decision to choose De La Rue, although Bradbury Wilkinson also continued to work for the Bank until the end of the Civil War in 1939.

Thomas De La Rue produced four issues, in January 1935, July 1935 (col. plate 18), August 1936 and March 1938, but only the first three were put into circulation. The last one coincided with the Civil War and the majority of the notes never arrived in Spain, but were held in a branch of the Bank in Paris. For obvious political reasons most of these notes were destroyed during and after the war. The De La Rue notes are of interest both for their excellent quality and because the Bank of Spain sent Spanish engravers to assist in their production; however, the designs did not differ significantly from those of Bradbury Wilkinson. The portraits of monarchs were removed and replaced with prominent historical figures, but the general concept of the notes was very similar.

The Civil War of 1936–9 at first brought about greater variety in the note production, but eventually Spanish banknotes were once again printed in Spain. During the Civil War the country was divided into two factions, and notes issued by the Republicans were printed in England by Bradbury Wilkinson and Thomas De La Rue, while the opposing forces had their notes supplied from Germany and Italy. In 1940, after the end of the Civil War, Bradbury Wilkinson approached the Franco regime, but the government turned them down on the grounds that they had previously worked for the Republic. At this point the new government decided to print the banknotes in Spain, and ever since then they have been commissioned from the Mint. Today the notes of the Bank of Spain still carry the imprint of the 'Fabrica Nacional de Moneda y Timbre' in Madrid, showing that they are made in their own country.

Notes

1. I would like to thank the British Museum and especially Virginia Hewitt for giving me the opportunity to prepare this paper.
2. For more information on these issues, see Tortella, T., 'The first banknotes issued in Spain: Banco Nacional de San Carlos (1782–1829)', in *Proceedings of the XIth International Numismatic Congress*, vol. IV, Louvain-la-Neuve 1993, pp. 185–8.
3. Here I can give only a general impression of this interesting period of Spanish note production, but there is an enormous amount of material on this subject in the archives of the Bank of Spain in Madrid, and it is available to anyone interested in knowing more about the history of English banknote printing for Spain. Moreover, a part of this material is in English – and the door to the archives is always open.
4. T.H. Saunders was in fact a paper manufacturer, but he took responsibility for the whole process of note manufacture for the Bank of Spain.
5. Although it is true that in general the Bank accepted the conditions set by Saunders, they always wanted to have control over the manufacturing process and initially the deputy

governor was sent to oversee every detail in the production, which in some cases lasted three or four months! Later other Bank employees of lower status were sent.

6. Unfortunately the letters do not name the engravers subcontracted by Saunders.

Bibliography

Banco de España, *Los billetes del Banco de España 1782–1979*, Madrid 1979.

Kranister, W., *The Moneymakers International*, Cambridge 1989, pp. 232–63.

Ruiz-Velez Frias, Florián, and Alentorn Vila, Jorge, *Catalogo del papel moneda español*, Madrid 1974.

1 (*below*) Banco Español de San Fernando, 500 reales, 1 March 1850, T.H. Saunders.

2 (*opposite, top*) Bank of Spain, 1,000 reales, 1 May 1956, T.H. Saunders and Perkins, Bacon & Co.

3 (*opposite, bottom*) Bank of Spain, 4,000 reales, 1 May 1862, T.H. Saunders

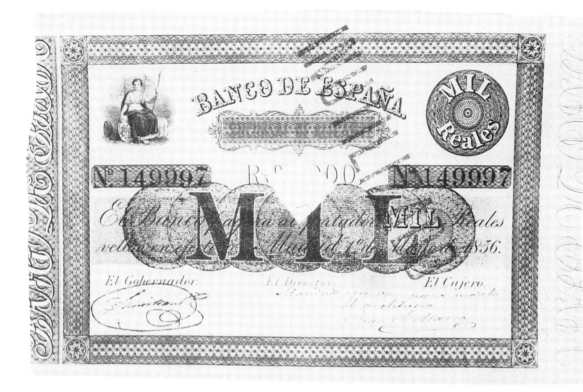

9

Late Qing paper money from Dianshizhai and other printing houses in Shanghai, 1905–1912

Helen Wang

In the 1980s the British Museum acquired over sixty private banknotes dating from the turn of the century to the beginning of the Republic of China in 1912. The notes were acquired mainly from two sources and include a high proportion of specimen notes, never intended for circulation, and of used notes in good condition. Although the original source of the notes is not known, their condition suggests that some may once have formed part of a printer's archive that has since been broken up.

To date, little research has been done on the private banknotes of this period. Very few of the private banks represented in the British Museum collection are listed in recent Chinese publications on Qing dynasty paper money, and then only with the briefest of explanation.[1]

Privately issued notes pose numerous problems. They were issued by a variety of organisations such as banks, pawnshops, mines and stores selling any kind of merchandise. The private banks were known to the foreign communities in China as native banks.[2] In general, the extent of their note circulation depended partly upon the reputation of the issuer, so that notes of a more reputable issuer would have a wider circulation, and partly upon the currency system of the region where the notes were issued, as this varied from region to region during the late Qing. Although there is plenty of information concerning the official banks and the paper money they issued, the Qing government appears to have made little attempt to manage the private issuers, content or at least tolerant at first that they were filling a much-needed gap in the traditional silver/cash system. The Qing government had in fact made use of the remittance facilities offered by the Shanxi banks, private banks whose status was enhanced by government patronage, and which were at one time the main medium of interprovincial trade. Yet with the growth of foreign commerce in China in the late nineteenth century the Shanxi banks were 'slowly giving up local business in favour of the local native banks, whom, in many instances, they helped to establish. To put it plainly, the native banks did local credits, mortgages, received deposits and took charge of such business as pertained to local trade.'[3] The nickname 'street notes' (*jie tie zi*) indicates that some notes, especially those of smaller issuers, would have been accepted only in a small area of the city where they were issued, sometimes only in one street.[4] The majority of privately issued notes are therefore not likely to have survived, and any records associated with the issuers are likely to be held in local rather than national archives. The problem of identification of notes and their issuers is further compounded when there is no indication of place-name on a banknote.

Despite these difficulties, there are eight notes in the British Museum collection which can be viewed as a small group, since they were all designed by the same artist, Wu Songqing, and printed in Shanghai, at various printing houses, during the years 1905 to 1912. Three of the notes were printed at Dianshizhai, and one at the Shenchang printing house, associated with Dianshizhai. Little is known about Wu Songqing or about the issuers of the notes; more is known about the printing houses, especially Dianshizhai, its publications and artists.

The Dianshizhai printing house was established in May 1884 by a British merchant, Ernest Major. Major was already an established businessman in Shanghai by then, with interests in tea, medicines and photographic supplies. He had also been building up a reputation in publishing – in 1872 he started the daily newspaper *Shenbao*, and in 1880 he took over the Shenchang printing house, followed by the Tongwen publishing house in 1884. An illustration of April 1887 shows three of Major's printing concerns side by side: Dianshizhai shuji (Dianshizhai Books), Shenchang shuhuashi (Shenchang Studio of Calligraphy and Painting), and Shenbaoguan shuji (Shenbaoguan Books).[5] The illustration is an advertisement offering printing services for books, lithographic reproduction, posters and maps, and boasts machinery imported from overseas.[6] A drawing by the most famous of the Dianshizhai artists, Wu Youru, shows the Dianshizhai printing workshop with its imported English lithographic presses, which worked on manpower.[7] Dianshizhai was one of the first printing houses in China to use lithographic techniques, which had first been introduced to China by missionaries for the mass production of religious pictures. The advertisement also promotes Dianshizhai's printed editions of classical works and pictures loved throughout the land for over a decade, and calls for proof-readers to apply for work, offering accommodation for employees, although expecting them to bring their own brushes and inkstones. Traditionally, illustrators and calligraphers tended to work within clans, and it may be that a foreign-owned organisation such as this offered more anonymous working conditions and the promise of more attractive opportunities in the international city of Shanghai.

The key publication emerging from Dianshizhai was the *Dianshizhai huabao* (*Dianshizhai Pictorial*). The first issue came out at the end of April 1884 and the last, no. 528, came out fourteen years later, in August 1898. Although Major, the founder and owner, was British, the editor-in-chief, Wu Youru, was Chinese and could therefore have been expected to know how to cater for the Chinese market. As van Briessen and Zürcher have both noted, Major's inspiration for the journal came from Western pictorials, such as the *Illustrated London News* (established 1842) and *The*

Graphic (established 1869).[8] It is worth noting, however, that although Wu Youru set up his own pictorial, *Feiying ge huabao*,[9] one year after Ernest Major decided to return to England in 1889, production of the *Dianshizhai huabao* continued until 1898.

The name of the printing house is a pun: it forms the first half of the four-character phase 'dian-shi-cheng-jin', literally, 'touch the stone, it turns to gold', a phrase thought to have originated in a supernatural story about immortals, but which has come to be used to describe someone who has the gift of turning bland words into literature. It was a perfect name for Major's new business venture, sure to be a success,[10] and especially apt for a printing house using lithographic presses to produce paper money.

However, most research relating to Dianshizhai has focused on the *Dianshizhai huabao*, and I have been unable to find any mention of their printing paper money. This suggests that the notes in the British Museum collection were not necessarily part of the well-known repertoire of Dianshizhai-printed classical texts but rather formed part of a commissioned trade ordered by private banks of which little documentation has survived or been studied. The seven-year period between the earliest and latest note in this group (1905–12), and the fact that they are the work of one artist, suggests that rather than being an experimental sideline, this commissioned trade was by then fairly well established. Given that the last issue of the *Dianshizhai huabao* was in August 1898 (after Major's departure and Wu Youru's independent venture), and the earliest date on the eight notes in the British Museum collection is 1905, it is perhaps reasonable to assume that Dianshizhai and its artists had to adapt to new lines of work, including the printing of paper money.

Although little is known about the issuers and the artists, closer observation of the notes themselves reveals a wealth of information. Details of the eight notes are given below in chronological order, and some are illustrated in the plates. The denominations are given in the terms used on the notes, which follow a system whereby 100×10-cash coins is equivalent to 1,000 cash which is equivalent to 1 string of cash.

1. For issue by the Lihe Bank, 1905 (BM C&M 1981-1-22-29) (fig. 1)

Dimensions and colour: 244×96 mm. Obverse design and text in black. Reverse design and text in green.
Obverse text (banking details): Issuer: *Lihe*. Location: *Hong pailou, Changsha* [in Hunan province]. Denomination: *Issue exactly one string of 'trade note' cash.* Instructions for use (below issuer): *The issuer holds no responsibility for lost notes;* (below serial number): *Exchangeable for silver coin at market value.* Serial number and date incomplete, no reign period indicated.
(complementing design): Prose piece, *Hou chu shi biao*, by Zhuge Liang (181–234). Production details: *In the first half of winter of the yisi year* [i.e. 1905] *of the Guangxu reign period, illustration by Wu Songqing, calligraphy by the owner of the Lihe Qianhao.*
Reverse text: *Changsha Lihe*. Production details: *Lithographic printing at the Five Colour Printing Bureau, in the Hucai Quarter, East Qipan Street, Shanghai.*

2. For issue by Yongquantai, 1905 (BM C&M 1984-6-5-8457) (frontispiece and fig. 2)

Dimensions and colour: 227×107 mm. Obverse design and text in blue. Reverse design and text in brown.

Obverse text (banking details): Issuer: *Yongquantai*. Location not indicated. Denomination: *On presentation of this note issue exactly 100 'value-10' copper coins.* Instructions for use (below serial number): *The issuer holds no responsibility for lost notes; exchangeable for silver coin;* (between issuer and banking details): *Beware of forgeries.* Serial number and date incomplete, no reign period indicated.

(complementing design): Prose piece, *Qian chi bi fu*, by S Shi (1037–1101). Production details: *On a bright morning in the yisi year* [i.e. 1905] *of the Guangxu reign period, calligraphy by the Yue Lake Fisherman of Leisure, illustration by [Wu] Songqing.*

Reverse text: *At the west entrance to the street market, on the south side facing north.*

3. [Issuer unknown], 1908 (BM C&M 1984-6-5-8448) (figs 3 and 4)

Dimensions and colour: 229×108 mm. Obverse design and text in blue. Reverse design and text in red.

Obverse text (banking details): Issuer, space left blank. Location: *Meng yi dajie* (Mengyi main street). Denomination: *On presentation of this note issue exactly 100 'value-10' copper coins.* Serial number and date incomplete, *Guangxu* period (1875–1908).

(complementing design): Prose piece, *Bian jian lun*, by Su Xun (1009–66). Production details: *Calligraphy by Feng Wushi, at the southern window of the guests' quarters, printed by the Dianshizhai Shuju on Dama Road, Shanghai, on an autumn day in the 34th year of the Guangxu period, wu shen* [i.e. 1908].

Reverse text: *For the owner, by [Wu] Songqing on an autumn day, wu shen* [i.e. 1908]. *[Seal of Wu] Song[qing].*

4. For issue by the Hengchang Bank, 1908 (BM C&M 1984-6-5-8460) (figs 5 and 6)

Dimensions and colour: 237×136 mm. Obverse design and text in blue. Reverse design and text in red.

Obverse text (banking details): Issuer: *Hengchang hao*. Location not indicated. Denomination: *On presentation of this note issue exactly 1000 cash.* Serial number and date incomplete, *Xuantong* period (1909–11).

(complementing design): Prose piece (incomplete), *Bei shan yi wen* by Kong Zhigui (447-501). Production details: *On a mid-autumn day in wu shen* [i.e. 1908] *calligraphy by Gu Yiting of Jiaxing, illustration by Wu Songqing of Jinkui, printed on commission by Dianshizhai Shuju, Shanghai.*

Reverse text: Prose piece, *Taohuayuanji* by Tao Yuanming (*c.* 370–427). Location of issuer is given in the four corners: *Suixi dajie* (Suixi main street).

5. For issue by the Qianshunxiang Bank, 1909–11 (BM C&M 1981-1-22-24) (figs 7 and 8)

Dimensions and colour: 206×115 mm. Obverse background in green, patterned frame in brown, design and text in black. Reverse design and text in orange.

Obverse text (banking details): Issuer: *Qianshunxiang qianzhuang*. Location: *Hunan*. The calligraphy of both issuer and location is in seal script. Denomination: *On presentation of this note issue exactly one string of cash*. Serial number: [incomplete] the character *Qing*, stamped in red ink, has been struck out with a black line. Instructions for use: *Bearers of notes that have been tampered with or have been found to be forgeries will be prosecuted*. Date: *Xuantong* period (1909–11).

Reverse text: The name of the issuer, *Qianshunxiang zhuang*, is given in the four corners of the note, written in a standard calligraphy. The panels above and below the two globes read *Eastern hemisphere* and *Western hemisphere*. The panel at the foot of the note gives the name of the artist and printer: *Illustration by Wu Songqing, printed at the Caowen shuju, Shanghai.*

6. For issue by the Yurui Bank, 1909–11 (BM C&M 1984-6-5-8463)

Dimensions and colour: 180×86 mm. Obverse design in black, central design (bank name, denomination, serial number, year) in black, characters *Xuantong* and other text in red. Reverse in green.

Obverse text (banking details): Issuer: *Yurui*. Location: *Nanchang, Jiangxi province*. Denomination: *On presentation of this note issue exactly 100 cash on the '95 dian'* [?] *standard*. Serial number and date: incomplete, *Xuantong* period (1909–11).

(complementing design): Prose piece, *Lan ting ji xu* by Wang Yizhi (321–79 or 303–61). Production details: *Illustration by Wu Songqing, five colour lithographic printing by Zhong yu shan fang, Shanghai.*

Reverse text: *Mianhua shi* (Cotton Market).

7. For issue by Tongshen, 1912 (BM C&M 1984-6-5-8458) (figs 9 and 10)

Dimensions and colour: 227×106 mm. Obverse upper design in black, lower design in blue, patterned frame in green, text in black. Reverse design and text in red.

Obverse text (banking details): Issuer: *Tongshen*. Location not indicated. Denomination: *On presentation of this note issue exactly 100 'value-10' copper coins*. Instructions for use: *Valid only upon presentation of this note, no personal favours*. Serial number and date incomplete, no reign period indicated.

(complementing design): Prose piece, *Jian Taizong shi si shu* by Wei Zheng (580–643). Followed by a second prose piece, *Shi shuo*, by Han Yu (768–824). Production details: *Illustration by Wu Songqing, printed by Dianshizhai, Shanghai.*

Reverse text: *The seven sages of the bamboo grove. Done in the 8th month of the ren zi year* [i.e. 1912], *for the owner of Tongshan by Wu Songqing, printed by Dianshizhai.* [Seal-mark of: Wu] *Songqing.*

8. [Issuer and date unknown] (BM C&M 1984-6-5-8449) (figs 11 and 12)

Dimensions and colour: 200×114 mm. Obverse upper design in red, lower design in green, text in black. Reverse in red.

Obverse text (banking details): Issuer: space left blank. Location not indicated. Denomination: *Present this note for issue of exactly* [blank space for denomination to be filled in]. Instructions for use: *Valid only upon presentation of this note, no personal favours.* Serial number and date: incomplete, reign period not indicated.

(complementing design): Prose piece, *Ge yan* by Zhu Xi (1130–1200). Production details: *Calligraphy by the Yue Lake Fisherman of Leisure, illustration by [Wu] Songqing, printed by Shenchang shushi.*

Reverse text: no text; design only.

Many of the notes immediately call to mind the characteristic features of the traditional design of Chinese paper money of the Qing dynasty, both government and private issues. The earliest surviving specimens issued by the Qing government are the Hubu guanpiao and Daqing baochao of the 1850s, during the reign of the Xianfeng emperor (1850–61). The earliest surviving specimen issued by a private organisation during the Qing dynasty dates to the reign of the Daoguang emperor (1821–50).

Both government and private issues were printed on paper, cut into rectangular strips and printed, usually in blue/black ink, to give a vertical note, on which the printed outline often tapers at the top to look like an unsealed envelope. The name of the issuer is written horizontally near the top of the note in large characters reading from right to left. Beneath it, a horizontal line separates the issuer's name from the key information in the tall rectangle below. This information reads vertically in columns, which are sometimes separated by fine lines. The denomination, often written in larger characters, lies down the centre, the serial number down the right-hand side, and the date down the left. Other information printed in the tall rectangle usually repeats the name or location of the issuer, or explains the conditions of use. The provision of blank spaces allowed the issuer to fill in by hand the serial number, date and, if not already printed, the denomination. This was not only for convenience; it also allowed the issuer to identify the handwriting if necessary at a later date. Finally, the seal marks of the issuer were stamped on the note.

The tall rectangle is always surrounded by a pictorial border. On the official notes issued by the Xianfeng emperor, there are in the top border two dragons chasing the pearl (symbolic of the sun), their bodies curling down the side borders into the clouds reaching down to mountains and sea at the foot of the note. The dragon is a symbol of imperial authority and appears on later issues of official paper money. It is not found on privately issued notes before the end of the empire. The mountains and sea are also symbols, found on the robes of officials at the imperial court, and together with the dragons and pearl may suggest a cosmic representation of the empire.[11]

On privately issued notes the borders are filled with scenes from well-known stories, or contain symbols and rebuses of good luck. Occasionally the pictorial border is replaced by a border of text. The earliest known issue with both a pictorial and a textual border dates to the end of the Xianfeng period, and in this case, the text frames the pictorial border.[12]

In addition to the traditional official and private banknotes circulating in China from the late nineteenth century, there was a growing number of notes issued by foreign banks for use in China. These notes are distinct from the traditional Chinese notes: they are horizontal in design, have bilingual inscriptions and very different design features, often associated with Western imperialism and the concept of banking on an international scale.[13] Elements from such notes were copied on later official and private Chinese issues, for example the use of the globes on Note 5 (fig. 8), showing the eastern and western hemispheres as seen on notes of the International Banking Corporation.

The eight notes in the British Museum collection were clearly made for private issuers, although none was ever put into circulation. Four notes give a reign period in the banking details of the central rectangle: one for the Guangxu period (1875–1908) and three for the Xuantong period (1909–11); the other four leave a space – printing neither a reign period nor Minguo (Republic) (1912–49) – or they print the single character *nian* (in the year of). There is sometimes an indication of date in the text complementing the obverse design, although this does not always correspond with the date given in the banking details, as in Note 4. The space normally giving the name of the issuer has been left blank on two notes (Notes 3 and 8), perhaps suggesting that these were sample designs which private issuers could select, or that it may have been a specification in the commission of the design that the issuer should supply the calligraphy or stamp to be inserted here.

Many of the scenes around the central rectangle may be derived from scenes from classical novels or Confucian texts, and have yet to be fully identified. The composition of the scenes is restricted to the narrow band framing the rectangle, usually about 12 mm wide, though as little as 9 mm in Note 1 (fig. 1), yet by using composition techniques found in traditional Chinese painting, the artist manages to create eight or more individual scenes with a sense of space. The scenes are usually separated by means of buildings, steps, mountains, ornamental garden rocks or trees, which are arranged to guide the observer's eyes in a zigzag down the note, thus making maximum use of the small space. The zigzag breaks up the back-, middle- and foregrounds with natural features that also serve to link scenes together. This technique combines well with the use of Chinese perspective, which does not limit the artist to one fixed vanishing point as in Western perspective, but allows for a more isometric representation of buildings and gives a feeling of depth to scenes of nature by twisting tree-branch behind tree-branch or contrasting flat stretches of water beside high mountains.

Wu Songqing uses these techniques well and seems to favour in particular the use of trees (Notes 1, 2, 3, 6, 7, 8), often using different species of tree to give a varying density of cover. In this way, branches of weeping willow can hang loosely, gnarled tree-trunks stand solidly, pine branches twist round with clusters of dense needles, and bamboo sway under lighter foliage allowing plenty of light through from behind. The trees are not only effective in terms of composition; many also have a symbolic significance. Bamboo is often the subject of ink paintings and a symbol of longevity. The pine and cypress are also symbolic of longevity and are often found together. Willow, a sign of spring, is used in the filial act of sweeping the ancestral graves at the Qingming Festival, and is believed to possess power over demons. It is fitting that the willow accompanies the scene of the young man carrying his elder on Note 2 (frontispiece; bottom left-hand corner). The trees on Note 3 (figs 3, 4) are aptly lush with leaves, separating the scenes with the young scholar – so often the hero of a Chinese romance – and the beautiful young woman.

The use of illustrative scenes from classical texts strongly suggests that these notes were created by artists with a wide repertoire of figurative and narrative scenes, perhaps following years of experience in book illustration, particularly of the 'well-loved classics' for which Dianshizhai was famous. If they were drawing to this tiny scale directly onto the stone slabs for lithography, as shown in Wu Youru's picture of the workshop, such expertise would be essential. The scenes on the obverse of Note 3 (fig. 3) are particularly engaging: the scholar relaxing with a good book in the pavilion in the shade of cool bamboo; the young woman drawing back the curtain of the window; the poor fellow's thoughts or dreams of the beautiful woman, envisaged in the clouds. The reverse of the note (fig. 4) continues the playful theme. Here again, there is a clear zigzag down the note, allowing a 'chapter' of ten scenes to evolve in a space little more than 13×6 cm. The narrative starts in the top left-hand corner with the scholar, playing the zither (qin) indoors. He pays a visit to a monastery/temple, welcomed through the doors by the bald monk or nun. He glances upon two young ladies of leisure (indicated by the very long sleeves), who have come ostensibly for religious purposes (indicated by the incense-burner on the stand). The scholar engages in conversation with one of the ladies. The ladies then talk together, first by the tree and then in one of the temple halls, before embarking upon a game of 'go' (weiqi) which the scholar views from his hiding place on the wall behind the tree. The final scene shows the scholar in relaxed conversation with one of the young ladies. The temple was one of the few places which respectable young ladies could visit by themselves; it was also a suitable place for eligible young scholars to spend time. Hence, temples and gardens frequently form the meeting ground, and sometimes playground, for romantic encounters, and similar scenes may have appeared in books printed by Dianshizhai. It is interesting that Zürcher notes criticism of malpractices in Buddhist monasteries and convents in the *Dianshizhai huabao*.[14] Although the last issue of *Dianshizhai huabao* predates this note by ten years, the supposed spotless reputation of the monasteries and temples clearly continued to be a subject of popular comment.

A more sedate scene is found on Note 7. The reverse design (fig. 10) shows the famous Seven Sages in the Bamboo Grove, a tale dating back to the third or fourth century. Again we see the zigzag created by the fences and the leaning bamboo, while the learned men take their time over calligraphy, admiring the scroll and, just arriving, the young boy with the zither. To remind us that this is paper money, the inscription on the scroll repeats the denomination in a shortened form. A similar scene is found at the top of the obverse (fig. 9): again there are mountains in the background, fencing, rocks and trees (cypress and pine, both symbols of longevity) and gentlemen at their calligraphy. Here the inscription on the scroll repeats the denomination word for word.

Calligraphy and scholars reappear in scenes on other notes, especially Note 1 where pairs of gentlemen appear in the robes of officialdom, with their books or playing 'go' (fig. 1). Unusually, each figure is named, but is yet to be identified.

The Eight Immortals are another recurring theme (on the obverse of Notes 1, 3, 4). They feature regularly in Chinese popular culture and are supposed to have the power 'of changing, by a species of stone which they have discovered, whatever they touch into gold'.[15] It is appropriate that they are found separating the banking details on Note 1, printed by Dianshizhai. (They appear at the top of Notes 3 and 4, figs 3 and 5). There is also a long history of a 'stone culture' in Chinese traditions, often linked with Daoist belief, and most famously in the novel, *The Story of the Stone*, by Cao Xueqin (d. *c.* 1764).

The themes mentioned above do not cover all the scenes pictured on the eight notes, but illustrate some of the very traditional elements of both classical and popular Chinese culture used on the paper money of this period. However, even on the notes of 1905, there are also elements of a newer, more international life. Notes 1 and 2 both show ships at the top of the obverse. Note 1 (fig. 1), with its wheel and cabins, may be typical of the passenger boats of the Yangtse River. The ship on Note 2 (frontispiece) is a sleeker vessel, proudly bearing the name of the issuer on its tallest flag, and on plainer water, composed of horizontal lines (perhaps in a more Western style).

Strong Western influence is seen on Note 8, in the train at the top of the obverse (fig. 11). The train not only shows the use of Western perspective, as it gradually diminishes in the background, but even portrays the driver and his passengers in Western clothes and hats. The confident Wu Songqing has even put his own name where we would expect to find the name of the train or the issuer. The reverse (fig. 12) shows a bold depiction of a foreigner with full beard and epaulettes waiting in impatient stance – his hands on his hips – as the clock reads just past twelve, in very foreign Roman numerals. The building is of Western style, with its dome, flag, arched windows, shutters and curved steps up to the entrance. A very similar building is found in the *Dianshizhai huabao*, perhaps suggesting more than coincidence, given that this note was printed by the Shenchang printing house.[16]

It is also interesting that although this note is the most Western in design, it maintains very traditional Chinese elements on the obverse (fig. 11). Even in the 4 mm border surrounding the banking details, Wu Songqing has depicted some of the most classical subjects of traditional Chinese painting, trees, flowers, birds and insects, many of which are symbolic: for example, narcissus (flower of the water immortal, good fortune), bamboo (longevity), lotus (sign of summer, admired for producing pure white flowers despite having roots thick in the mud, associated with Buddhist rebirth), pine (longevity), chrysanthemum (sign of autumn, associated with a life of ease and retirement from public office). It was clearly very important to maintain such traditional Chinese features in the design of paper money.

Other narrow borders (often only 2–3 mm wide) show plum blossom and pointed foliage against a crackled background (reverses of Notes 2, 4, 7), a gourd pattern (obverses of Notes 2, 8), a cloud pattern (reverses of Notes 2, 6), geometric designs, striations and, in the wider borders, more expansive floral decorative patterns. The texts bordering the figurative scenes are mostly taken from famous pieces of classical prose, dating from as early as the fourth century AD, and would have been instantly recognisable to an educated person. They are philosophical in nature, contemplating the good things of the past, and encouraging a life of virtue and morals – the scenes on Note 3 in particular suggest a Confucian approach to life, that is, to live according to the principles of virtue. Many of these famous prose pieces may be found in such classical anthologies as the twelve-volume *Guwen guanzhi*, containing literature from the Eastern Zhou to the late Ming, compiled by Wu Chucai and Wu Diaohou during the Kangxi period (1662–1722). This came to be a very popular anthology, and editions may well have been printed at Dianshizhai.

Note 5 differs in design from the other seven, and follows the design of an officially issued note of Hunan province.[17] In the centre at the top of the obverse (fig. 7) is the sun with a facing phoenix on either side. In the middle of the sun is the character *ri* (sun). Zigzag lines flare out from around the sun, behind the two phoenixes and clouds to left, right and below the sun. The bodies and feathery tails of the phoenixes are lengthened to fill the vertical space down the outsides of the central panel. The cloud pattern below the sun forms the background for the decorative arrangement of the issuer's name and location and continues down the outsides of the central panel behind the phoenix tails. Below the central panel crashing waves rise in the centre and at each side, almost meeting the end-feathers of the phoenix tails. The obverse design of this note copies almost exactly the officially issued note, but replaces the official issuer's name with that of the private issuer, and the original two dragons (symbol of the emperor) with the two phoenixes. It is interesting that the obverse of the note adheres so strictly to the traditional design of the official issue, even retaining the seal script calligraphy, yet substitutes elements which evoke strongly the changes that were taking place in the contemporary Chinese world. The Xuantong emperor was a small child at this time, and the Empress Dowager is known to have held sway. The Chinese phoenix comprises both pheasant and peacock, and is a symbol associated with empresses. It is also a symbol of rebirth, perhaps used here in association with the imminent overthrow of the Qing dynasty and the establishment of the Republic.

In contrast, the reverse design (fig. 8) suggests a much more modern world, with two globes showing the eastern and western hemispheres (which strangely do not name China), and the use of more standard fluent styles of calligraphy. On the obverse, when single characters are used in the serial numbers on Chinese notes they are often taken from *The Thousand Character Classic (Qian zi wen)*, which does not include the character *qing*, used here. It is possible that the striking out of the character *qing* may be connected in some way with the imminent overthrow of the Qing in 1911, although this would have been a very dangerous note to possess if it was ever issued as paper money. The creased folds on the note render it less pristine than the other seven – perhaps it may have been used for some other purpose?

Although few in number, this small group of notes confirms that Dianshizhai, and other printing houses in Shanghai, were printing paper money during the years 1905 to 1912, that is, at the end of the Qing dynasty and in the first year of the Republic. These notes were all designed by Wu Songqing, an artist from Jinkui in Jiangsu. Some of the notes also give the name of the calligrapher, which may suggest either that the owner preferred to supply his own, or that Wu Songqing concentrated on illustration. One possible explanation is that Wu may have come from a clan of illustrators – he was certainly well versed in the traditional styles of illustration such as those found in Chinese painting and novels and in popular culture and religion – rather than from a background that promoted calligraphy, traditionally associated with the well-educated, but this can only be speculation. More research is needed on print-making and illustration of this period before a fuller picture of his life may be drawn. Similarly, more research is needed on the regional economies of the catchment area of Shanghai during this period, and on the key players in the issue and movement of money – official, foreign and private banks, and local and regional business magnates – at a time of enormous change in the history of China.

Acknowledgements

I would like to thank Joe Cribb, Andrew Lo, Wang Tao and Zhang Hongxin for their encouragement and suggestions during the preparation of this paper, and Bill Barrett, who brought the banknotes to the British Museum.

Notes

1. Many new publications on Chinese numismatics have appeared over the last few years. However, those authors writing on paper money have tended, naturally, to focus on the major banks first, leaving aside the private issuers.
2. For details of the different terms for these organisations, see McElderry 1976, King 1965, Wu 1993.
3. Wagel 1915, pp. 156–7.
4. Yang 1952, pp. 69–70.
5. Briessen 1977, p. 18.
6. Peter Bower and Du Weisheng (of Beijing Library) have kindly examined the eight notes and suggest that two may have been printed on imported paper, the rest on Chinese. Bower pointed out that although 'Japanese vellum' (imitation Chinese/Japanese paper) was fashionable in Europe then, more research is needed to establish if it was economically viable for this style of European-made paper to be imported into Shanghai at this time.
7. Reproduced on the front cover of Zheng 1958, and in Briessen 1977, p. 15.
8. Briessen 1977, p. 14; Zürcher 1994, p. 110.
9. Chen 1990, p. 113.
10. Zürcher 1994, pp. 109–10: 'The *Dianshizhai huabao* was a typical product of the nineteenth-century "China coast culture" – it was basically a hybrid, and that no doubt accounts for its extraordinary success.' See Lu Xun 1957, pp. 229–30 for his comments on Wu Youru's illustrations showing a lack of understanding of foreign things.
11. Wilson 1990, pl. 2.
12. Wu 1993, p. 152, no. 83, note issued by the Fengyuqing Bank.
13. Zhongguo renmin yinhang jinrong yanjiusuo 1992.
14. Zürcher 1994, p. 132.
15. Williams 1973, p. 124.
16. Zheng 1958, p. 109.
17. Wu 1993, p. 193, no. 126.

Bibliography

Briessen, F. van, *Shanghai-Bildzeitung 1884–1898 – Eine Illustrierte aus dem China des ausgehenden 19. Jahrhunderts*, Zurich 1977.

Chen, Gaowen, 'Shanghai yi bao kao (xu)', in *Xinwen yanjiu ziliao* (49), Beijing 1990.

Dai, Jianbing, *Zhongguo jindai zhibi*, Beijing 1993.

Jenkins, Penny, 'Vexed by Vellum Papers', in *The Paper Conservator*, vol. 16, 1992.

King, F.F., *Money and Monetary Policy in China 1845–1895*, Harvard 1965.

Lu, Wenzhao (ed.), *Guwen guanzhi*, Shanghai 1948.

Lu, Xun, 'Shanghai wenyi zhi yi bie', in *Lu Xun quanji (di si juan)*, Beijing 1957, pp. 228–41.

McElderry, A.L., *Shanghai Old-Style Banks (ch'ien-chuang) 1800–1935*, Michigan 1976.

Shanghai, *Shanghai zhinan, Guide to Shanghai, A Chinese Directory of the Port*, 11th edn, (revised), Shanghai 1920.

Wagel, S.R., *Chinese Currency and Banking*. Shanghai 1915.

Williams, C.A.S., *Outlines of Chinese Symbolism* (repr. of 1931 Peiping edition), Taipei 1973.

Wilson, Verity, *Qing Costume*, 2nd edn, London 1990.

Wu, Chouzhong (ed.), *Zhongguo lidai huobi daxi (7)*, Shanghai 1993.

Yang, Lien-sheng, *Money and Credit in China*, Harvard 1952.

Zhang, Jinglu (ed.), *Zhongguo chuban shiliao bu bian*, Beijing 1957.

Zheng, Wei (ed.), *Dianshizhai huabao shishi huaxuan*, Beijing 1958.

Zhongguo renmin yinhang jinrong yanjiusuo (ed.), *Zibenzhuyi guojia zai jiu Zhongguo faxing he liutong de huobi* (Money issued by capitalist nations for circulation in old China), Beijing 1992.

Zürcher, Erik, 'Middle-class ambivalence: religious attitudes in the Dianshizhai Huabao', in *Etudes Chinoises*, Printemps-Automne, vol. XIII, no. 1–2, 1994, pp. 109–43.

1 Note 1, Lihe Bank, 1905 (obverse).

2 Note 2, Yongquantai, 1905
(reverse).

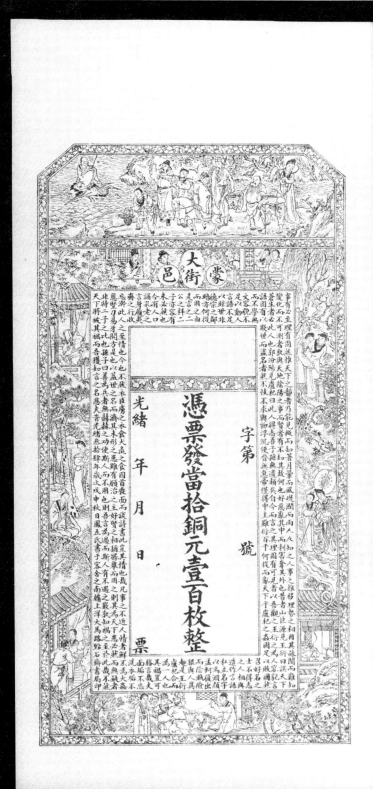

3 Note 3, unknown issuer, 1908
(obverse)

4 Note 3, unknown issuer, 1908
  (reverse).

110

5 Note 4, Hengchang
  Bank, 1908
  (obverse).

晉太原中武陵人捕魚為業緣溪行忘路之遠近忽逢桃花林夾岸數百步中無雜樹芳草鮮美落英繽紛漁人甚異之復前行欲窮其林林盡水源便得一山山有小口髣髴若有光便捨船從口入初極狹纔通人復行數十步豁然開朗土地平曠屋舍儼然有良田美池桑竹之屬阡陌交通雞犬相聞其中往來種作男女衣著悉如外人黃髮垂髫並怡然自樂見漁人乃大驚問所從來具答之便要還家設酒殺雞作食村中聞有此人咸來問訊自云先世避秦時亂率妻子邑人來此絕境不復出焉遂與外人間隔問今是何世乃不知有漢無論魏晉此人一一為具言所聞皆歎惋餘人各復延至其家皆出酒食停數日辭去此中人語云不足為外人道也既出得其船便扶向路處處誌之及郡下詣太守說如此太守即遣人隨其往尋向所誌遂迷不復得路南陽劉子驥高尚士也聞之欣然規往未果尋病終後遂無問津者

6 Note 4, Hengchang Bank, 1908 (reverse).

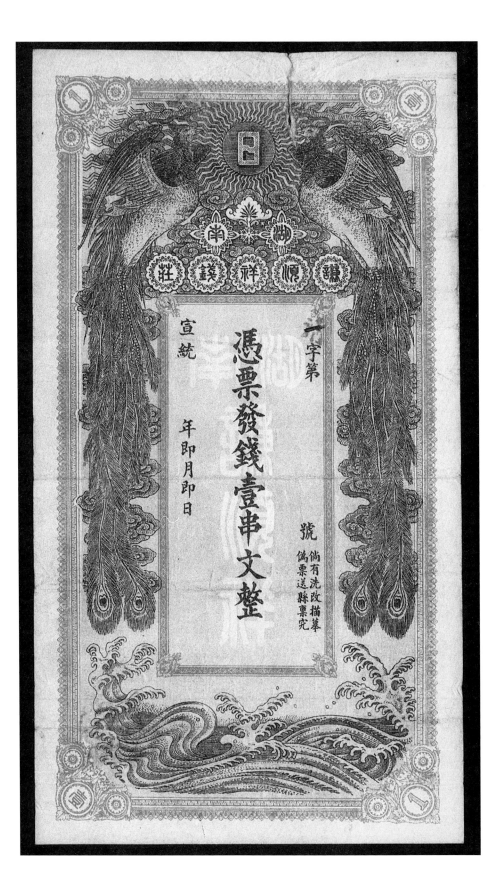

7 Note 5,
Qianshunxiang
Bank, 1909–11
(obverse).

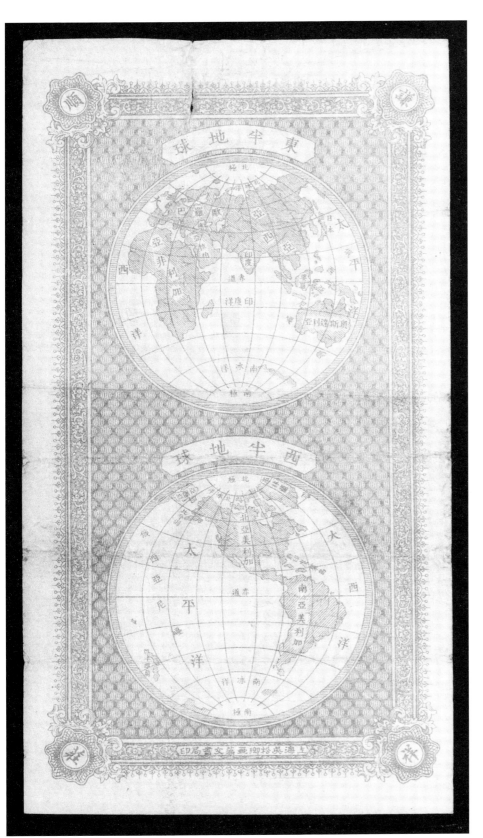

8 Note 5,
Qianshunxiang
Bank, 1909–11
(reverse).

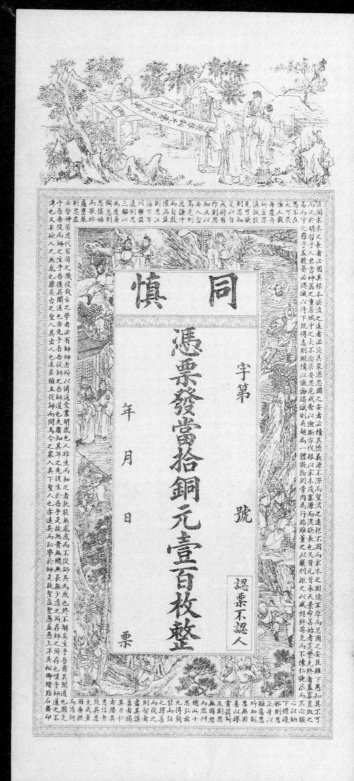

9 Note 7, Tongshen, 1912 (obverse).

10   Note 7, Tongshen, 1912 (reverse).

116

11 Note 8, issuer and
date unknown
(obverse).

12 Note 8, issuer and
date unknown
(reverse).

10

Surviving images, forgotten peoples: Native Americans, women, and African Americans on United States obsolete banknotes

Richard G. Doty

For Americans of the nineteenth century, private banknotes represented a vital ingredient in the economic life of the Republic. In a nation chronically short of specie (and the raw material from which to create it), the currency circulated by chartered banks – and railroads, insurance companies, land developers, even hotels and lyceums – meant the difference between stagnation and capitalisation, between bad times and good. For Americans of the twentieth century, these private banknotes represent something altogether different but equally valuable: they provide one of the clearest views of themselves when young. The images they present can suggest, with a more than photographic intensity, not how Americans actually were, but how they wished to appear, to themselves and others, both then and in times to come. If the notes are approached with this in mind, a great deal can be learned.

For example, one can discover how the dominant portion of the population felt about several other important but essentially powerless parts of the American whole. These groups were large and deeply rooted, contributing primary ingredients to the uniqueness, the prosperity, the very existence of the country, and they formed a constant pictorial feature of the currency produced and circulated at the time. This is ironic, for all three groups existed mainly outside the money economy, which in itself suggests that their portrayal on banknotes might be less than strictly accurate. Native Americans, women, and African Americans appeared on private banknotes because the dominant group in society deemed them interesting and important, but the timing and nature of their introduction to American currency were conditioned by two other, prosaic considerations – the danger of forgery and the desire for abundant money.

These desiderata were simultaneously addressed and achieved by the New England inventor Jacob Perkins and members of his circle. The method by which success was obtained involved a transfer process, wherein images and fancywork could be engraved on a soft steel plate, hardened, and used to impress a raised version of the same design onto a soft steel cylinder or roll. Once the latter had been hardened, it could in turn be employed to transfer any number of identical, intaglio designs onto any number of soft steel plates, and these, when hardened, could be used for printing.

The vignette rolls were fairly small, because the transfer process involved in their creation and replication required immense pressure. This meant that a working printing plate could not be created from a single cylinder, in a single process. Several rolls would be required to place a portrait here, an allegory there, a lathework medallion with a denomination somewhere else. And even then, much handwork would remain, for the name of the issuing bank would probably be engraved by hand, as would anything else so specialised that nothing like it existed in the printer's menu of possibilities. But the very limitations of size, the fact that plates could not be created in a single process, gave the methodology great flexibility. By the 1830s, images could be cropped, expanded, or retouched at will, strung across a note to tell a story or point out a moral. The difficulty of engraving a custom-made image or portrait encouraged the printers to use and re-use what they already possessed with minor, or even major, changes. In sum, the form taken by the banknotes reflected the limitations and possibilities of the technology used to produce them.

With minor exceptions, that technology had been perfected by the early 1820s. What had begun as a simple means of making safe and abundant paper money could now be employed in additional activities, including the dissemination of particular views of particular people, impressions of their work and preferred role as defined by a white, male-dominated society.

Native Americans had become popular subjects for inclusion on the notes by the end of the 1820s, a popularity they would maintain through the remaining years of the private banknote. But the manner in which they were portrayed, the impression of them which the bankers and their printers hoped to create, evolved in several different directions across time.

First, there was the depiction of historical figures, a tendency particularly evident in the 1830s. The nature of one such attempt says more about the dominant society than those it put on its money, for the same image was used for three different leaders from three different Native American tribes – Tecumseh, Washtenaw, and Schenda – presumably with the idea that native peoples and their chiefs were interchangeable. The same image was also employed by a number of Midwestern banks without a designation of the subject, further strengthening the conviction that the vignette was 'stock' rather than a sincere effort at accurate delineation.

Attempts were also made to depict real events, especially as improved artistry and technology created the possibility of more ambitious vignettes in the 1840s and 1850s. A note from Florence, Nebraska of 1858 shows one such scene, an odd image of Native Americans fleeing from Pilgrim contact (fig. 1), while a slightly earlier note from New

York recorded a similar encounter between two dubious warriors and an American sailor. But Native Americans were commonly viewed as existing beyond or outside the white man's idea of time and when displayed on banknotes, this attribute could be implied in a number of ways.

It was most often expressed by placing Native Americans in what whites imagined were typical activities and poses. Their skills as hunters received particular notice, and a stock image of a male waiting in ambush was replicated and manipulated in several different ways. Buffalo-hunting and the horse which made it possible were becoming popular images by the late 1830s, and some magnificent renditions of the activity were being offered by the mid-1850s – particularly on notes from places where the memory or presence of pursuer and pursued were still strong. The importance of the canoe also received mention: one of the earliest and most successful engravings of this mode of transportation appeared on a $3 bill of 1831 from the appropriately named Mohawk Bank of New York. Later images were often less realistic and more fanciful, with canoes and their occupants reduced to objects of decoration or didactics. In this, as in most other connections between Native Americans and banknotes, those who commissioned them and those who produced them could never quite leave well enough alone. The people on the notes must be made to tell a story which was flattering to the dominant community and which would bolster the image that the printers, bankers, and businessmen had of themselves, as opposed to the ostensible subjects of the notes.

This could be effected in various ways. One of the most popular methods featured Native Americans encountering Progress, and reacting to it with a number of predictable, reassuring poses. In many cases, the encounter with Progress might appear to be a simple, realistic depiction of a Native American – except when viewed more closely. On a Nebraska note of the 1850s, a dismounted figure seems to be gazing into the distance, perhaps at his comrades at a buffalo-hunt, but he may rather be seeing a railroad for the first time – and the white technology behind it, which will soon change his way of life (fig. 2). This image is the spiritual heir of an earlier vignette (on a note from Freehold, New Jersey, of 1855) which pictures a standing male either greeting or symbolically barring Progress, as typified by the train.

Very commonly, the subject will gaze down from a high spot on a bustling scene beneath, a scene in which he – or sometimes she – can only be an onlooker, never a participant. The figure may express a regal disdain for the nineteenth century, as on another Nebraska note of the late 1850s: the seated warrior's back is imperiously turned on the busy scene beneath him. A bill printed forty years earlier presented the same concept in a much more economical way: the man in the canoe paddled his craft away from the white man's covered bridge (fig. 3).

So far, so good – although the images are unlikely, the native is presented with the new and remains wedded to the old out of choice. But those who called for, designed, and used the notes were not content to leave the matter there: the Native American must also come to realise the error of his choice and desire to remake himself in the white man's image.

His wife might help him reach the proper conclusion. There is a marvellously self-serving engraving of a seated Native American male, gazing at a plough and log cabin, apparently annoyed by his inability to grasp either concept. The image was popular, and it appeared on notes from a variety of places along the eastern seaboard in the 1850s. But an Indiana bank interposed a mother and child in the scene so that Native Americans now encourage each other to abandon old ways in favour of new! A similar treatment is found on an issue from the Fontenelle Bank of Bellevue, Nebraska. We might not side today with the imploring female in the tableau, but then the definition of Progress has changed a good deal since she made her appeal (fig. 4).

Another version of the story begins as simple allegory, without racial overtones. One white female instructs another in the virtues of agriculture – in this case, the pineapple, whose cultivation in Kinderhook, New York must surely have inspired comment at the time (fig. 5). Alter the standing figure's skin and dress, however, and we now have a white instructing a Native American in the joys of settled agriculture (fig. 6)! This image is self-serving, of course, but it suggests a useful improvement, the introduction of an exciting new food product to an otherwise bland native diet.

By now, we are moving beyond even a nodding acquaintance with reality, yet the bankers and printers were still not finished. Native Americans could be used as elements of heraldry. An 1851 note from the Bank of Salisbury, Maryland, depicts them in this way, posed unfavourably with a similar group of whites on the other side of the national shield. This type of allegorical comparison was another common way of hammering home the point about Native American inferiority versus white superiority. Native Americans could also be employed as simple props: an attractive maiden is used in this way on a $10 bill from Memphis, bearing a huge ear of maize in one hand, an 'X' for the denomination in the other.

This note leads us to the final types of Native American images on early banknotes, the vaguely erotic and the frankly surreal. The producers and issuers of banknotes in the nineteenth century had an ambiguous relationship with what they would have called the 'fair sex'. We shall soon see what happened when they depicted white women on notes, but let us dwell first on Native American women. These were often depicted with as little drapery as was consistent with community standards. A coy maiden with bow and arrow was a popular image around 1860; a contemporaneous image from Texas showed more flesh while managing the same healthy disrespect for reality (fig. 7). For the truly surreal, though, another two images must cap the repertoire. First, we have a young maiden crossing a stream – perhaps the artist had just finished reading the saga of Eliza in *Uncle Tom's Cabin* (fig. 8). Second, there is a reappearance of the canoe with a brave-to-be sitting in his own tiny boat with a duck's head for a prow. But if you look very closely in the distance to the left, you will see the dim outlines of a city: young as he is, this child too knows what he wants and what he fears (fig. 9).

White American women suffered as greatly at the hands of engravers and bankers as did their Native American sisters. Members of both groups first appeared on the notes at about the same time, and many of the earliest depictions of white women ranged from the cloying to something approaching the pornographic, though they failed actually to cross that line because their subjects were either mythological or allegorical and hence were not supposed to be fully or even partially clothed. A pair of such images, both from the 1830s (figs 10, 11) will suffice to illustrate the point. Though this genre persisted down to the end of the private banknote itself, it was overshadowed after 1840 by somewhat more believable, and more fully clothed, depictions, whose lack of nudity was amply compensated for by other elements. Sweet-faced maidens, with or without doves, were in vogue as were pale young women of an 'interesting' mien. These images and many others suggested how the dominant socio-economic group wanted to regard women. Reality was otherwise, and some of the notes paid homage to that fact.

These latter portrayed historical figures – not as often as white males, of course, but with some regularity. Most of the females chosen had better-known husbands or connections with more famous males, and that was an obvious criterion for their inclusion on the currency. Martha Washington fell into this category, as did Rachel Jackson, Kate Sevier, and Dolley Madison. Others depicted on the notes arrived there by their own merits. Jenny Lind was one such success story while another was Henriette Sontag, an opera singer who made the first of several American tours in 1852, and who was immortalised on a Connecticut note not long thereafter. However, most women on money enjoyed a subordinate reality, placed there to show an activity, or point out a moral. Their images were manipulated by those who prepared and circulated the bills they graced, but truth peeps out at us from place to place, if we know how and where to look for it.

While Native Americans might exist beyond the popular conception of time and place, white women most certainly did not. They functioned in conjunction with men, a point constantly made on the notes. They work, for instance, with their husbands, brothers and sons in a variety of farming activities, but a telling point recurs: they are frequently depicted seeing to the comforts of their menfolk, taking their own ease only after these needs have been satisfied. And yet the general imagery is one of camaraderie and affection, as a farmer leans over a gate to speak to his wife, or a courting couple takes a stroll once the work is done. The engravers created, and the bankers circulated, imagery that would reinforce the status quo and the popular perception of reality in the relationship of women and men, but who is to say that what they perceived and what they disseminated was so very far off the mark?

What were women's specific roles in life as seen by the notes? As we might expect, motherhood was a primary function, and the money of the day displayed a number of scenes of mothers and their children, rendered with delicacy and grace. Here is Woman at her perceived best, nurturer and instructor. At times the depiction veers towards the overtly sentimental, as with an image for a bank in Medford, New Jersey. A seated woman, an American Madonna, if you will, tenderly cradles her child, oblivious to their surroundings. Those surroundings are interesting, though – on this note a satisfying agricultural scene relates to the central figures. It was later altered to a harbour view which made no sense whatever, prepared at the behest of a bank in Troy, New York. Motherhood did not change all that much until our own lifetimes, and many of us will view these images with a sense of remembrance.

Of course, woman's work went beyond motherhood. It still centred on the farm, and the currency abounds in images of women harvesting grain, including one on a bill from a Delaware bank, whose pineapple suggests that we have seen something like it before (fig. 12). Vignettes connecting women with other crops are less common, but there is at least one note with a scene of a tobacco harvest and another which features hops. Other farmwork depicted on early notes included the care and feeding of livestock and fowl, as well as churning – from a simple image in 1828 to something far more elaborate by 1855. These scenes connected with dairying lead us to one of the most frequently depicted professions on early notes – that of the milkmaid.

From the unadorned testimony of the money, milking cows must have been the American growth industry of the nineteenth century. We see milkmaids, their pails, and distinctive three-legged stools everywhere – singly (fig. 13), in pairs, and in groups, but almost never performing their appointed labour – milking cows. Assuming that the Republic was not surfeited with a glut of milkmaids, we may conclude that this group of images was so prevalent upon the notes because its members represented freshness, youthfulness and innocence, attributes which those in command feared the nation was losing as it moved into the industrial age.

Banknotes proclaim that such a movement was indeed taking place, and that women had an essential role to play. They are seen making thread in a Paterson, New Jersey note of the 1820s; they weave it into cloth on a Millville (the name is appropriate!), New Jersey issue of the late 1850s. Other notes add allegory to representations of manufacturing, creating a satisfying scene of industrial plenty, as on a $5 bill of the Bank of Cohoes, New York (fig. 14). Women's work was hardly confined to factory and field: they also did piece-work at home, along with their men. But the factory scenes point the way, for they are our first indication that the role of women might be expanding away from tradition and towards the present, represented by the wage economy of the Industrial Revolution. Now representatives of one of those groups so frequently featured on America's money were actually beginning to use it!

Members of the third group illustrated on notes had few such prospects at the time. These were African Americans. While a single instance is known of the depiction of free people of colour on an obsolete note (fig. 15), the anomalous nature of free blacks is underscored by the very fact that only one such image is known to have existed. Throughout the era of the private note, most African Americans were slaves, and it was in this capacity that they were shown on the money.

They were occasionally included on banknotes back to the 1820s, but these instances were widely scattered and always allegorical. By the time their depiction achieved a modest vogue among Southern banks, that section was rather on the defensive about the institution under which these people laboured, and banknote printers were caught somewhat off guard, being asked for distinctive African American images when they had none in stock.

Fortunately, the nature of their technology came to the printers' rescue. Northern-orientated images could be retouched and the difficulty temporarily resolved. So a white farm worker from a New York note (fig. 16) might have his complexion darkened and his clothing tattered – and emerge as a slave in Virginia (fig. 17). A wheat-harvesting scene from a bank in Michigan could be extensively reworked to reappear as a cotton-picking vignette for a bank in North Carolina. In time that reworked image could and did acquire a distinctly Southern identity, making a final, crude appearance on a wartime bill from Thomasville, Georgia.

Northern printers eventually acquired a repertory of Southern vignettes, at the centre of which 'King Cotton' remained. We can trace the product's progress from field to wharf, along with the anonymous stories of those who grew, carried and sent it on its way. Certain images lasted longer than others: two slaves at work chopping cotton appeared on a note from the Bank of Savannah, issued a few days before Georgia threw in its lot with the Southern Confederacy. That new entity reused the image on its first bills of credit, issued from Montgomery but printed in New York and smuggled south early in 1861. The Confederacy was soon reproducing the scene by lithographic means on Southern-printed $100 bills. Another transfer from Northern to insurgent printers portrayed a slave picking the crop. We see him bent at his work, his carrying baskets at the ready, but a comparison of the Northern original and its Southern descendant would have raised troubling questions for the aspiring nation – if this was the best its technology could muster, trouble most certainly lay ahead.

While cotton dominates, other crops – and those who tended them – are also found on Southern currency. Cane cutters are seen on notes from the Central Bank of Nashville, Tennessee, while a piece from Howardsville, Virginia introduces the juxtaposition of slavery and tobacco.

Thus far, all the images discussed have connected servitude to agriculture in one way or another – an accurate reflection of the Southern section's primary economic and social concerns. References to Southern industry are very sparse even in conjunction with free workers and virtually unknown in connection with slaves. But there is at least one such vignette, seen on a $4 bill from the Bank of Yanceyville, North Carolina, dating from the mid-1850s. Yanceyville was situated in tobacco country, and what we see here is a scene from a factory dedicated to the preparation of that commodity (fig. 18). Nevertheless, Southern notes cannot offer the multiplicity of industrial images seen on Northern issues, a hint at problems to come in the event of a war between the two halves of the nation.

White and black, master and slave, lived in unavoidable contact with each other but while an owner might work alongside his servant, there was never the slightest doubt of who was in command. As elsewhere, images on nineteenth-century banknotes reinforced the 'natural' order of things – at least from the standpoint of those on the top and middle rungs of the ladder. As with the images of Native Americans, Northern printers and their Southern customers could never quite leave well enough alone. By the mid-1850s, the debate over slavery was acquiring a force which would finally lead to war. In the North, outcry over the institution grew; under attack, the South replied with those weapons at its disposal, aiming its message at citizens of both sections, and one of the guns in its arsenal was the content of its money. The image of the slave was now romanticised. He became an object of affectionate folklore, an Uncle Remus who drowsed at his tasks (fig. 19), an amiable chucklehead who remained in bondage for his own good. He sang at his work, happy with his lot. The apotheosis of this trend was reached in a vignette produced at the end of the 1850s. One of the most evocative images in the entire story of the private banknote, the fact that it graced bills from half a dozen institutions suggests that it struck a deeply responsive chord then as now, if for different reasons. We see a slave mother and child. She smilingly holds her baby while the laughing infant toys with a branch of cotton – the plaything that enslaves them both (fig. 20). By the time this image was gracing Southern notes, the two sections of the country were sliding towards war. That conflict, which both sides hoped could be kept of short duration and restricted to a limited debate, perversely refused to perform according to plan. When it was over, neither of the two sides would be instantly recognisable from the vantage point of 1860, the last 'normal', prewar year.

The North was now more industrial than ever before, the balance between field and factory having definitively shifted in favour of the latter. The South saw an institution uprooted which had been simultaneously economic, social, and racial – and no one yet knew what might arise in its place. At bottom and immutably, the power of the national government had increased while that of the states had diminished. The leaders of the triumphant Union might be diffident in taking their new, national authority to most of its logical points of conclusion, but they did make one move which directly interests us: needing money to prosecute the war, the government of Abraham Lincoln found a portion of it by forcing private, note-issuing banks into a federal banking system, wherein their assets were used to purchase war bonds, and their purely private circulating paper was discouraged and finally taxed out of existence. Now conformity of design would be the order of the day, and the marvellous scenes on the earlier notes would begin their journey from private money into public memory.

Bibliography

AFFLECK, CHARLES J., *The Obsolete Paper Money of Virginia*, 2 vols, Virginia Numismatic Association 1968.

ANDERSEN, GUNNAR, *Banknotes*, Copenhagen 1975. The best brief text I have seen on the technology behind the banknote, with good coverage on Jacob Perkins and the other pioneers.

HAXBY, JAMES, *Standard Catalog of United States Obsolete Bank Notes, 1782–1866*, 4 vols, Iola, Wisconsin 1988. Some information on banking histories; profusely illustrated.

HOOBER, RICHARD R., *Pennsylvania Obsolete Notes and Scrip*, Society of Paper Money Collectors, Inc. 1985. The S.P.M.C. is the major collector group for obsolete American currency, and its ambitious publication project, embracing notes and scrip of each state, is now nearing conclusion. The quality of these publications is somewhat variable, but all represent a major improvement over earlier tests. Hoober's is one of the best.

TYLER, FRANCINE, 'The Angel in the Factory: Images of Women Workers Engraved on Ante-Bellum Bank Notes', in *Imprint. Journal of the American Historical Print Collectors Society*, 19, no. 1, Fairfield, Connecticut, spring 1994. Discusses narrative scenes on banknotes of women at work, placing them within the context of social history.

WISMER, D.C., *New York Descriptive List of Obsolete Paper Money*, Federalsburg, Maryland 1931. Still useful, but soon to be superseded by the S.P.M.C. publication on New York.

In addition, those interested are invited to consult a Krause publication, a monthly newspaper called *Bank Note Reporter*, the contents of which (while theoretically covering all United States paper) have traditionally concentrated on obsolete, Confederate, and Southern states materials. Also, I write from time to time about obsolete notes I have found in the National Numismatic Collection which are unlisted elsewhere.

Opposite page

1 (*top*) Bank of Florence, $1, 1858.

2 (*bottom*) Western Exchange Fire & Marine Insurance Co. (Omaha, Nebraska), $2, 1857.

3 (*above left*) Susquehanna Bridge Co. (Unadilla, New York), $1 1817.

4 (*above right*) Fontenelle Bank, $3, 1856.

5 (*below left*) Union Bank (Kinderhook, New York), $2, 1850s.

6 (*below right*) Bank of the Republic (Washington, DC), $10, 1852.

SCOE, HARRIS

TWO YEARS FROM D

100

THREE

12 (*left*) Bank of Milford (Milford, Delaware), $3, 1854.

13 (*below*) Bank of Orange County (Goshen, New York), $1, *c.* 1850.

14 (*bottom*) Bank of Cohoes, $5, *c.* 1860.

Opposite page

7 (*top left*) Briscoe, Harris & Co. (Harrisburg, Texas), $3, 1861.

8 (*top right*) Town of Cedar Falls (Iowa), $1, 1858.

9 (*centre left*) Fairfield County Bank (Westport, Connecticut), $1, *c.* 1840.

10 (*bottom left*) Mechanics' Bank of Augusta (Augusta, Georgia), $100, 1854.

11 (*bottom right*) Tecumseh Bank (Tecumseh, Michigan), $3, 1838.

18 Bank of Yanceyville,
    $4, 1850s. (Courtesy
    of Hugh Shull,
    Camden, South
    Carolina)

19 Manufacturers' Bank
    (Macon, Georgia),
    $20, 1862.

Opposite page

15 (*top*) Bank of
    Catasauqua
    (Pennsylvania), $10,
    c. 1857.

16 (*bottom left*) Farmers
    Bank of Onondaga
    (Onondaga Valley,
    New York), $1, 1852.

17 (*bottom right*) Bank of
    Howardsville
    (Howardsville,
    Virginia), $50, 1861.

20 Bank of the
    Commonwealth
    (Richmond, Virginia),
    $50, 1858.

11

Agents of culture and nationalism: the Confederate Treasury and Confederate currency

Guy R. Swanson

The American Civil War (1861–5) continues to spark much discussion and scholarship in the United States – both in the North and in the South – and in countries throughout the world. The Museum of the Confederacy routinely answers research enquiries from the United States, the United Kingdom, Australia, Canada, Germany, the Netherlands, and occasionally questions from countries such as Poland and India. Some of the enquiries concern the current collecting value of Confederate financial instruments, and how to sell them for United States dollars. Evidently the old adage occasionally heard throughout the American South, 'Save your Confederate money, boys, the South will rise again,' still has a ring of truth.

The American Civil War was caused by many forces that were all related to each other. Those forces are best understood as a fabric, all woven together, and they include, but are not limited to, political questions concerning state sovereignty versus federal authority, slavery, economics, agriculture in the South versus industry in the North, the shift of political power from Southern states to Northern and Western states, and growing differences in culture.[1]

In an effort to preserve what they held dear to their very existence, the states in the American South seceded from the Union in late 1860 and early 1861, and formed the Confederate States of America.[2] The Confederate Constitution was modelled (with adjustments) on the United States Constitution. The new government resembled its Federal counterpart and had three branches: legislative, executive and judicial. The capital was Montgomery, Alabama, from February until June 1861, when the government moved to Richmond, Virginia.[3]

The Confederate government had a Treasury Department, which was within the executive branch, headed by a secretary of the treasury who reported to the president. Two men served as treasury secretary for the Confederacy, Christopher G. Memminger from 1861 to 1864, and George Trenholm from 1864 to 1865. The Treasury Department was responsible for all fiscal concerns, especially the collection and disbursement of funds. In 1861 Congress authorised the department to issue $1 million in paper currency, and by 1864 the issue had reached $800 million. Despite an attempt to reduce the quantity of money in circulation in 1864, the level was once again at $800 million in 1865.[4]

The design, printing, and distribution of the paper currency was administered by the Treasury Department's Treasury Note Bureau. Gold, silver and other precious metals were quickly hoarded at the start of the war, and even though the Confederacy captured three United States mints, the Treasury Department never issued coins for circulation.[5]

The Treasury Note Bureau had two divisions, one located in Columbia, South Carolina, which administered the printing of the notes, and another in Richmond, which supervised the signing, clipping, numbering, packing and shipping of the notes. Throughout much of the war the division in Richmond required a staff of nearly three hundred clerks, most of them women, to sign twice and then number over eighty million notes. The Richmond branch moved to Columbia in late 1864.[6]

The Treasury Note Bureau did not have an engraving and printing office of its own and it contracted with various independent printers to produce the currency. In early 1861 there were only eight security engravers in the Confederate States. Three of them had experience engraving steel plates, but they were affiliated with firms located principally in the North. The Treasury Department closely monitored the activities of the various firms, for some of them were more interested in their own profits than in serving the Confederacy.[7] Before the outbreak of war the first Confederate currency was manufactured in New York City by the National Bank Note Company in March 1861. The notes were subsequently issued from the first Confederate capital in Montgomery. They are familiarly known as 'Montgomeries' and are the most handsome and striking of all Confederate notes.[8] For example, a $1000 note of 1861 balances elegant lettering and security printing with portraits of John C. Calhoun, United States senator, and Andrew Jackson, president of the United States (fig. 1).

After the fighting began, the Treasury Department was obliged to arrange contracts for the production of its currency with firms located within the Confederacy.[9] Due to the shortage of skilled engravers and the demand for millions of notes, lithography generally took the place of the fine steel engraving used for the first issues. Two of the better-known firms used were Hoyer & Ludwig of Richmond, and Keatinge and Ball of Columbia. The Confederate government also used agents stationed in the British Isles to engage the assistance of Scottish lithographers.[10]

The images and designs used on Confederate currency in 1861 and 1862 depicted neo-classical symbols evoking the ancient civilisations of Greece and Rome, as well as scenes representing the early American Republic and its growth into nationhood. For example, classical concepts of commerce and democracy were mingled with portraits of several ante-bellum American statesmen. These statesmen represented the ideals from which Confederates thought the United States had deviated by the start of the war, and there were Confederates who had been alive when Southerners such as George Washington, John C. Calhoun and Andrew Jackson had served the United States. In addition, Confederate currency is remarkable for the number of designs featuring women, black people, American Indians, and one prominent Confederate statesman who was a Jew.[11] The examples illustrated here indicate the variety of images on Confederate notes: various female allegories and a statue of George Washington (fig. 2), the diverse forces of John C. Calhoun, African Americans hoeing cotton and Columbia holding a wreath of victory (fig. 3), and figures of authority such as soldiers of the Confederate army, Lucy Holcombe Pickens (wife of the governor of South Carolina) and Secretary of War George Wythe Randolph (fig. 4).

The printers of Confederate money often lifted the designs from various private banknotes already in circulation throughout the North and the South. They also used readily available standard engravings or photographic images for their models. Because of the differences in clarity between the currency that was engraved and that produced by lithography, as well as the inability of the Treasury Department to monitor the use of the designs, a dangerous problem arose: Confederate notes were susceptible to forgery.[12]

In the autumn of 1862, therefore, the Confederate Treasury took action to combat counterfeiting by sponsoring a contest for new currency designs among the firms that printed currency, encouraging the use of original artwork. This effort to control effectively the use of designs was intended both to slow the activities of counterfeiters and to streamline the process of producing the notes.[13] However, in organising the contest the Treasury Department also created a means of publicising Confederate culture and nationalism. At the start of the war, treasury officials had not routinely discussed how paper money could instil culture and nationalism, but when this notion arose along with the attempt to end the counterfeiting problem it greatly helped the Confederacy towards defining itself as a nation.[14]

Currency passed through the hands of tens of thousands of people and thus provided the opportunity of evoking a chosen Confederate image. Illustrated newspapers, such as *Harper's Weekly* and *Frank Leslie's Illustrated Newspaper*, had recently come into their own in the United States, and in the Confederacy similar publications, such as *The Southern Illustrated News* and *Southern Punch*, were just emerging. Photography had changed from an expensive process using metals and chemicals, inaccessible to many individuals, to an inexpensive process using paper and chemicals, more accessible to all. But although illustrated newspapers and photography were important mediums, such vehicles of information were still available only to comparatively few citizens. Paper currency therefore became an effective tool with which to educate Confederates about their country.[15]

The winning entries from the Treasury Department's contest were submitted by Edward Keatinge and George Dunn, and, although some existing designs were continued, new currency was issued in December 1862. Images from the classical past and the early years of American history were augmented by designs that focused more on defining the Confederacy for its own citizens, as well as for those in the United

States and foreign nations. The new currency celebrated the American South and its eighty-year evolution culminating in the Confederate States of America. The notes featured portraits of individuals who represented the current leadership of the Confederacy (fig. 5) and scenes depicting what was important to Confederate life, such as commercial activity associated with the railroad or shipping on the high seas, architecture, the military (fig. 6), and hopes for the future.[16] A stirring combination of patriotic images appeared on the $500 note issued in 1864, a memorial tribute to Lieutenant-General Thomas J. ('Stonewall') Jackson, whose portrait appears facing the second national pattern Confederate flag and a modified version of the Great Seal of the Confederacy (fig. 7). If the Confederacy had won independence, its currency would surely have featured portraits of military leaders such as Generals Robert E. Lee, J.E.B. Stuart, and Nathan Bedford Forrest, as well as scenes of great military victories. Notes would probably have continued to depict both agrarian society and emerging industries, and without question images of Confederate political leaders would have endured as prominent features.[17]

The notion of paper money defining or expressing culture and nationalism is not a new one, and evidence of this role can be found on early notes from emerging countries and issues in the modern age, on which monarchs, national figures and other patriotic images help to define for a country's citizens who they are and for what they stand.[18] In the 1860s, the Confederacy was engaged in a war to maintain its independence, and the many political and military concerns facing the Confederate government influenced decisions concerning the images featured on its paper currency. The extent to which the Treasury Department effectively used its currency for other than strictly financial purposes is in fact quite remarkable.

The men and women of the mid-nineteenth-century American South were deeply conscious of images and symbols, and the meaning they extracted from them was an important component of their everyday lives. The currency of the Confederate States of America thus endures as a lively and imaginative reflection of how Southerners saw themselves and the storm-cradled nation for which they vainly sacrificed so much.

Acknowledgements

The author gratefully acknowledges the assistance of Douglas B. Ball, New York City; Mary Rebecca Barrett, Brevard, North Carolina; Richard G. Doty, Smithsonian Institution; Virginia H. Hewitt, the British Museum; Corrine P. Hudgins, the Museum of the Confederacy; Ludwell H. Johnson III, the College of William and Mary; Robin E. Reed, the Museum of the Confederacy; and James C. Ruehrmund, Richmond, Virginia. The currency illustrations are of material from the George W. Ball Collection. They and the others are courtesy of the Eleanor S. Brockenbrough Library, the Museum of the Confederacy, Richmond, Virginia. All photography is by Katherine Wetzel of Richmond, Virginia.

Notes

1. For additional information see the appropriate chapters in the following works: William J. Cooper, Jr., and Thomas E. Terrill, *The American South: A History*, New York 1990; E. Merton Coulter, *The Confederate States of America 1861–1865*, Baton Rouge, Louisiana, 1950; Clement Eaton, *A History of the Southern Confederacy*, New York 1954; Emory M. Thomas, *The Confederate Nation: 1861–1865*, New York 1979; and Frank E. Vandiver, *Their Tattered Flags: The Epic of the Confederacy*, New York 1970.

2. Listed in their order of secession the states that once formed the Confederate States of America are: South Carolina, Mississippi, Florida, Alabama, Georgia, Louisiana, Texas, Virginia, Tennessee, Arkansas and North Carolina. Kentucky and Missouri had rival Confederate and Unionist state governments, but were occupied by United States troops during most of the war.

3. For a readily accessible copy of the Constitution of the Confederate States of America see Thomas, op. cit., pp. 307–22.

4. Douglas B. Ball, 'Treasury Department', in Richard N. Current (ed.), *Encyclopedia of the Confederacy*, 4 vols, New York 1993, vol. 4, pp. 1614–16.

5. Ibid.; Ball, 'Currency', in Current, op. cit., vol. 1, pp. 433–8.

6. Ball, 'Treasury Department'.

7. Ball, 'Currency'.

8. Ibid.

9. As reference points for the outbreak of hostilities in 1861, the Confederacy attacked Fort Sumter, the United States Army installation located in Charleston Harbour, South Carolina, on 12 April; it surrendered on 14 April. The first major battle between Confederate States and United States armies took place on 21 July 1861 at Manassas Junction, Virginia, and is known as the First Battle of Manassas or the First Battle of Bull Run.

10. Ball, 'Currency'.

11. For portraits and other images used on Confederate currency see Grover C. Criswell, Jr., *Confederate and Southern States Currency: A Descriptive Listing, Including Rarity and Values*, 4th edn, Port Clinton, Ohio 1992; Gene Hessler, *The Engraver's Line: An Encyclopedia of Paper Money and Postage Stamp Art*, Port Clinton, Ohio 1993. The woman and the Jewish statesman were Lucy Holcombe Pickens, wife of South Carolina Governor Francis Wilkinson Pickens, and Judah P. Benjamin, who held various positions in the Confederate cabinet, most notably as Secretary of State. Richard G. Doty, 'Surviving images, forgotten peoples: Native Americans, women and African Americans on United States obsolete banknotes', pp. 117–31 in this volume, surveys the ways in which these various groups were depicted on private banknotes.

12. Ball, 'Currency'; Criswell, op. cit.

13. Ball, 'Currency'.

14. See Edward C. Elmore to Christopher G. Memminger, 6 March 1861, as cited in Richard Cecil Todd, *Confederate Finance*, Athens, Georgia 1954, pp. 77–8.

15. For additional facts see Cooper and Terrill, op. cit., p. 260; Eaton, op. cit., p. 227; Thomas, op. cit., p. 28; Vandiver, op. cit., p. 209; and the appropriate chapters in William Crawford, *The Keepers of Light: A History and Working Guide to Early Photographic Processes*, Dobbs Ferry, New York 1979 and Floyd Rinhart and Marion Rinhart, *The American Daguerreotype*, Athens, Georgia 1981.

16. Ball, 'Currency'; Criswell, op. cit.

17. As reference points for the fall of the Confederacy, General Robert E. Lee surrendered the Army of Northern Virginia at Appomattox Court House, Virginia on 9 April 1865; General Joseph E. Johnston surrendered the Army of Tennessee on 26 April near Durham, North Carolina; and President Jefferson Davis was captured on 10 May near Irwinville, Georgia.

18. For other discussions on this theme, see for example Willibald Kranister, *The Money Makers International*, Cambridge 1989, pp. 172–201; Virginia Hewitt, *Beauty and the Banknote: Images of Women on Paper Money*, London 1994; and articles in the present volume by Teresa Tortella, Helen Wang, Richard G. Doty, Tuukka Talvio and Virginia Hewitt.

1 Confederate States of America, $1,000, 1861 Montgomery issue.

2 Confederate States of America, $5, 1861.

3 Confederate States of America, $100, 1862.

4 Confederate States of America, $100, 1863. The design was first issued in 1862.

5 Confederate States of America, $50, 1864, featuring a portrait of the Confederate President, Jefferson Davis.

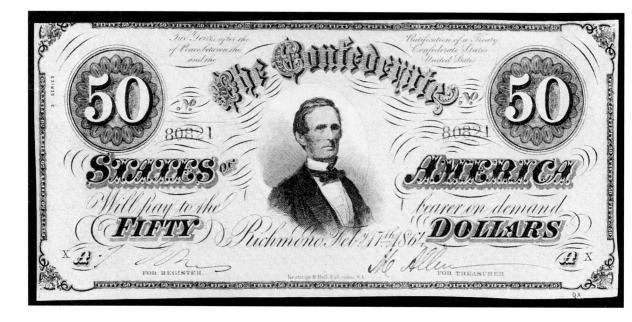

6 Confederate States of America, $10, 1864. The portrait is of Secretary of State Robert M.T. Hunter.

7 Confederate States of America, $500, 1864.

12

'Something characteristic of our land': Eliel Saarinen as a banknote designer

Tuukka Talvio

In the first decades of this century, the architect Eliel Saarinen designed two series of banknotes for the Bank of Finland. Some of his designs were used for over thirty years, until the 1950s. They have often been illustrated and commented on in publications dealing with banknotes, but outside Finland they have seldom been appreciated as the work of an artist who also made a major contribution to the architecture of his time.

Saarinen was born in 1873 at Rantasalmi in eastern Finland. He spent his childhood in the Russian province of Ingria near St Petersburg, where his father was the rector of a Finnish congregation. After studying architecture in Helsinki, in 1897 he founded a partnership with two other young architects, Herman Gesellius and Armas Lindgren. Their best-known works include the National Museum of Finland (1905–12). In 1904 Saarinen was chosen as the architect of the Helsinki railway station, and four years later he won the competition for the Finnish Parliament House, which however could not yet be built. In 1906 he participated in the competition for the Palace of Peace at The Hague, and in 1922 he received second prize in the competition for the Chicago Tribune Tower.

Saarinen's early works were conceived in a National Romantic style, which included neo-medieval elements, but he later developed a more classical and monumental, even grandiose, idiom. After participating successfully in several international competitions, in 1923 he moved permanently to the United States, where Cranbrook in Michigan became his new home. He died at Cranbrook in 1950.[1] Outside Finland, Saarinen's son, the architect Eero Saarinen (1910–61), is nowadays better known than his father. His works include many public buildings in the United States and Europe, among them the American Embassy in London.

Although Finland did not become an independent country until 1917, it had its own banknotes from 1811 and its own currency, the *mark*, from 1860.[2] The banknotes were printed first locally and then in St Petersburg, Berlin and Copenhagen, until in

1885 the Bank of Finland founded its own printing house in Helsinki. In 1897–8, a new series of notes was produced in co-operation with the British printers Bradbury, Wilkinson & Co. The fronts of the notes were printed in London and the backs in Helsinki. These notes display a remarkable series of allegorical figures which give the impression that Finland was already an independent country (fig. 1). At the turn of the century the Russian government began, however, to tighten its grip.

In 1907 the Bank of Finland decided to issue a new 1,000 mark note and at the same time to renew the whole series. The reasons were mainly technical: the printing colours used by Bradbury, Wilkinson & Co. had caused problems and it was apparently also felt that there was no longer any need for foreign expertise. Very likely there was a political motivation too, for it was hoped that the iconography of the new notes would be politically more neutral. In order to obtain 'artistically satisfactory' designs for the new notes, a general competition was announced. A prestigious jury was appointed to judge the results, which, however, proved to be very disappointing. Some forty designs were submitted, but none was considered good enough. Two well-known artists, Saarinen and the painter Akseli Gallen-Kallela, were now approached personally. Only Saarinen sent his design by the deadline, and he was given the commission. It is not surprising that he was asked, for he was known for his attention to detail and his fine drawings.

To judge from the sketches and drawings preserved in the archives of the Museum of Architecture and the Bank of Finland in Helsinki, Saarinen's original idea for the 1,000 mark note did not differ much from the final design. It shows on the back a typical Finnish landscape of a lake and islands seen through the branches of a huge spruce. On the front, economic life is symbolised by two standing figures holding the attributes of trade and industry (fig. 2). Similar pairs of male figures appear also on several of Saarinen's architectural designs of the period. His first drawings for the smaller notes also included symbolic figures of standing men as their central motif. The jury does not seem to have considered this motif worthy of such repetition, and Saarinen was given the advice that the designs for the banknotes should convey 'something more characteristic of our land'.

The final series consisted of seven notes with motifs depicting the Finnish landscape and various economic activities, such as fishing (5 marks), animal husbandry (10 marks), forestry (20 marks), seafaring (50 marks), agriculture (100 marks) and industry (500 and 1,000 marks). The style is decorative and strongly influenced by Art Nouveau, with finely drawn details based mainly on botanical forms. There are no portraits and nothing related to political institutions, with the exception of the two small coats of arms of the Russian Empire and the Grand Duchy of Finland.

The notes were printed in Helsinki and put into circulation in 1909. They seem to have been more popular than the Bradbury Wilkinson series, and were used until the events of 1918 made a renewal of the banknotes necessary. Early in 1918, a civil war broke out, and the 'Red' forces seized control of the Bank and its printing house. After the victory of the 'Whites' a few months later the notes issued by the revolutionary government were declared illegal, but as they could be distinguished from legal notes only by their serial numbers, the situation was difficult. The printing of the 1909 series was at first continued with changed colours, and the planning of a wholly new series was begun. Saarinen was formally engaged for the project in the spring of 1919, but he is said already to have started the work in 1918.[3] The new notes were authorised by the government in November 1922.

The backs of the 1922 series have much in common with the earlier notes: their principal motif is a conifer tree, pine or spruce, which since the 1860s had often been used as a national symbol on Finnish banknotes. On the smaller notes the tree motif also appears on the front. The decorative borders are reminiscent of Art Nouveau, already by 1920 rather antiquated.

The most remarkable element in the series was, however, the groups of nude figures on the front of the four largest notes (100–1,000 marks; figs 3, 4). These figures had caused much discussion among the bank supervisors. Until then there had been few human figures on Finnish banknotes, but now suddenly there was a whole procession of naked bodies. The final verdict was positive. As one writer has remarked: '. . . little by little the public got accustomed to the new notes. From a technical point of view they did not meet the requirements of specialists, but their artistic design and the ideological content of their imagery has made them generally popular'. By ideological content the writer meant 'an optimistic faith in the future'.[4]

If we look for models for Saarinen's designs, they are as difficult to find as in the case of the 1909 series. Nude figures are, of course, relatively common on banknotes. The Austrian expert in security graphics, Franz von Salzmann, had already in the 1830s favoured the use of mildly erotic illustrations in order that they should arrest the attention of the public and thus contribute to the detection of forgeries.[5] Saarinen may well have known von Salzmann's ideas through one of the bank directors who had visited Berlin and Vienna to study the technique of security printing. However, his groups of nudes have no obvious parallels, and we may also surmise that they were not primarily inspired by von Salzmann's theories from the 1830s.

The early drafts (figs 5–7) which are kept in the archives of the Museum of Architecture in Helsinki give us some idea of how Saarinen worked on his designs. As we have seen, the 1909 series had been practically void of human figures. Now Saarinen seems to have gone to the other extreme, for all the drafts for the larger notes show a group of people as the main component of the obverse side. In the first drafts the figures represent the various occupations and classes of society, as can be seen from their garments. Amongst them can be found, for example, an architect holding the model of a building which looks like the National Museum (fig. 5). Such depictions of the people in their everyday occupations were not uncommon on banknotes after the First World War.

What gave Saarinen's figures their originality was his bold idea of stripping them of their clothes. The late Oleg Tavaststjerna, who seems to be the only one to have written about Saarinen's early designs, has suggested that he simply wanted to remove class distinctions from his renderings of the Finnish people.[6] This point is well worth making, but it is not quite accurate: after all, most of the people on the notes can still be identified as farmers and workers. Undoubtedly the artistic and ideological background of Saarinen's nudes is more complex than this.

As Kenneth Clark notes in *The Nude*, the nude is an art form in itself, invented by the Greeks. Points of comparison for Saarinen's nudes are not difficult to find in paintings. It has been pointed out, for example, that the train of people moving towards the sunrise of a summer morning on the 1,000 mark note (figs 6, 7) has affinities with two frescoes in Tampere Cathedral, especially *The Procession of the Blessed* by Magnus Enckell (1907). However, knowing the early stages of Saarinen's designs we must come to the conclusion that the affinities in question are accidental or secondary. And even if we could find the prototypes for Saarinen's banknote designs in such paintings, it might not help us much, considering the special function of banknotes.

A more fruitful approach would seem to be to examine the designs from an ideological point of view. Banknotes were at that time issued in Finland only by the national bank, and their imagery was clearly meant to express national values. In 1919, Finland was a very young nation, recently out of a civil war, and very much in need of ideas and symbols which would unify the different classes of society. In banknote design, historical motifs – and especially portraits of national heroes – have traditionally had this function.

As an architect, Saarinen had by now turned his back on history, and it was only natural that he would also want to express modern ideas in his other designs. One such idea was belief in the vitality of the native race. There are examples of an idealisation of the people on the banknotes of several countries in the 1920s (for example, Estonia, Germany, the Netherlands, Switzerland), and it seems natural to include Saarinen's notes in the same category. His artistic solutions were original, but the ideological content of his designs appears to be rather typical of the time.

In Finland a parallel for the designs can be found in the public works of the sculptor Wäinö Aaltonen. An art historian has characterised Aaltonen's work from the 1920s and 1930s by saying that he 'created the image of a brave and athletic Nordic race, whose introvert nature conceals a tender soul and often also something typical of the ancient Greeks, the spirit of Hellas.'[7] As regards Wäinö Aaltonen it is also interesting to note that in 1930 he won a competition for a group of sculptures which were to be placed in the assembly room of the new Parliament House in Helsinki. All were nude figures symbolising the Finnish people. Several parliamentarians wanted them to be removed, but over the years they gradually became a part of the national imagery, in the same way as the 1922 banknote series.

One element in the idealisation of the race was the emphasis on sports. In the 1920s physical culture was often linked with 'naturism'. A well-known Finnish author, Olavi Paavolainen, wrote in 1929, 'The present cult of nudity is not merely an exceptional phenomenon which will soon be over, it is one of the basic features of life, as it was in the ancient world'. Another quotation from 1929 states, 'As regards the beauty of the human body, the athletic people of Finland can certainly compete with any other nation in Europe'.[8] Saarinen's nudes antedate these statements by nearly ten years. Although his work does not seem to have much to do with the world of sports, the prevailing interest in a healthy outdoor life quite certainly contributed to their popularity.

The 1922 series underwent several changes in the colouring, paper and water-mark. In 1940, a 5,000 mark note designed by Aarne Karjalainen was added to it, and in 1945 the 100 and 50 mark notes were replaced by new types drawn by Signe Hammarsten-Jansson. On the 1,000 and 500 mark notes, however, Saarinen's designs were used until a completely new series was introduced in 1955, nearly half a century after he had begun his work for the Bank of Finland.

The final verdict on Saarinen's banknote designs must be left for posterity. It will probably not differ much from what was already said in 1922 by one of the bank supervisors: Saarinen's banknotes were designed to appeal to 'a refined taste'.[9]

Notes

1. For presentation of Saarinen's life and work see M. Hausen, K. Mikkola, A.-L. Amberg and T. Valto, *Eliel Saarinen. Projects 1896–1923*, Helsinki 1990; also in Finnish: *Eliel Saarinen. Suomen aika.*

2. For information about Finnish paper money see T. Talvio, *The Coins and Banknotes of Finland*, Helsinki 1987. A more detailed presentation with references can be found in the second Finnish edition of the work, *Suomen rahat*, Helsinki 1993.

3. O. Tavaststjerna, 'Eliel Saarinen ja vuoden 1922 setelisarja', *Numismaatikko*, 1977, no. 1, pp. 3–7, at p. 7.

4. K. Kivialho in *Suomen kotimaiset setelityypit 1809–1951*, Helsinki 1952, p. 12; also in Swedish: *Inhemska sedeltyper i Finland 1809–1951.*

5. See W. Kranister, *The Moneymakers International*, Cambridge 1989, p. 111.

6. Tavaststjerna, op. cit., p. 4.

7. A. Reitala in *Suomen kulttuurihistoria*, III, Porvoo 1982, p. 437.

8. Both quotations come from an exhibition brochure, *20-luvun kasvot*, published by the Finnish Academy of Art, Helsinki 1972.

9. Kivialho, op. cit.

1 Bank of Finland, 500 marks, 1898 series, designed by Bradbury, Wilkinson & Co.

2 Bank of Finland, 1,000 marks, 1909 series, designed by Eliel Saarinen.

3   Bank of Finland, 100 marks, 1922 series,
    designed by Eliel Saarinen.

5   Early draft by Saarinen for the 100 mark note in
    the 1922 series.

4   Bank of Finland, 500 marks, 1922 series, designed by Eliel Saarinen.

6 Early draft by Saarinen for the 1,000 mark note in the 1922 series, showing clothed figures.

7 Saarinen's draft for the 1,000 mark note of 1922, with nude figures.

13

A legend tumbles down: the gypsy on the Banco de México five peso note printed by the American Bank Note Company

Elsa Lizalde Chavez

Recent history is seldom written objectively, partly because passions frequently blind the protagonists whose pens are responsible for the majority of these chronicles, and partly because many documents, sometimes confidential, do not see public light until many years after the events they record. Nevertheless, a characteristic of the Mexican individual is his tendency to speculate over certain unknown issues that he hears about frequently from 'first-hand and absolutely trustworthy sources'. To this information he adds a little more of his own until he creates a story that, due to its elaboration, becomes so credible that it is sometimes printed and thus passed on from generation to generation, eventually becoming a legend. Besides this, human nature is prone to gossip, even though it is prohibited by good manners and social conventions. The truth is that not only are we willing to believe 'what is said' by our politicians, but also to magnify it. Such was the case with the first banknote issued by the Banco de México, S. A., or Bank of Mexico, on its foundation in 1925.

As the country was then just beginning to get out of the successive convulsions provoked by the revolutionary movement, the new governments were determined not just to reconstruct the country but to build a new one. The economic situation was critical. The system of federal banks established in the late nineteenth century under President Porfirio Diaz had cracked, since the usurper Victoriano Huerta had seized the metallic reserves, and various institutions had been forced to flood the country with unsecured paper money. Added to these problems, the confusion caused by the note issues of different revolutionary groups prompted the government to seek a way out of the political, economic and social problems which afflicted the country. The decision during the presidency of Plutarco Elias Calles to establish a central note-issuing bank was therefore part of a wider process of economic reform which transcended questions solely of banking.

The idea of creating such a bank in Mexico was not new. President Calles had appointed as Minister of Finance Alberto J. Pani, who had already participated in the former administration as Secretary of Foreign Relations, after joining the Constitutionalists at the side of Carranza.[1] In the midst of the revolutionary movement, Pani had proposed the establishment of a note-issuing bank to Carranza, but he was not put in charge of this ill-fated project. Instead he had to try to rescue it, for when the coalition of the Constitutionalist Army disintegrated into factions, the Northern Division Chief, General Francisco Villa,[2] not only seized the presses and the notes already printed but also arrested all the employees of the printing works. Commissioned by Carranza, Pani negotiated with him to return the presses and to free the employees. At the happy ending of this difficult task – and to the surprise of Pani, who, knowing the customary aggression of the Northern Division Chief, feared for his life – Villa asked for his opinion about a project which he 'had cherished long ago', which was about to be set in motion and which everyone praised: the foundation, in Chihuahua, of an issuing bank. 'He showed me the bank note specimens', wrote Pani, 'I don't remember if they were already printed or if the American Bank Note Company of New York was going to print them.'[3] He went on, 'I declared myself against his idea and I must recognise that even when I objected to an idea that Villa was enthusiastic about he didn't get angry.' Indeed he listened with interest to Pani's explanation of the evils a plurality of issues could bring, as had occurred during the Porfirio Diaz administration, and of the advantage of waiting until the revolution succeeded before establishing an issuing bank.

Villa therefore declared that, 'If when the Revolution reaches Mexico City and ends the administration of the traitor Huerta, Don Venustiano [Carranza] doesn't establish a Central Bank as you say, I will establish it.' In fact, the bank was not established either by Villa, who failed in his Conventionalist adventure and was later defeated by General Obregon, or by Carranza, even though during his presidency the constitution ordered the founding of such a bank. Pani observed, 'I never thought that I could be the Secretary of Finance and Public Credit who, under the Presidency of General Calles, would establish eleven years later, the Bank of Mexico, S.A., that Pancho Villa had dreamed of' (fig. 1).[4]

The enthusiasm that Calles showed towards the project of the issuing bank had long been evident. He entertained no doubts at all concerning the establishment of such an institution even though it would involve a fundamental reform of banking and a series of economic adjustments. Pani recorded that 'the national gold reserves were approaching, towards the end of August 1925, 45 million pesos. With this sum and the healthy portion of the Monetary Commission's portfolio it was possible to establish the issuing bank.'[15] So the Bank of Mexico was born, thanks to the efforts of co-founders such as Elias S.A. de Lima and Manuel Morin. On 1 September 1925, complying with the provisions of an act decreed on 25 August of the same year, the Bank's doors opened on the premises formerly occupied by the Banco de Londres y México, the first private issuing bank to be established in the country during the Second Empire (fig. 2). According to Section VI of its Articles of Incorporation, the Bank of Mexico 'was founded mainly to issue money and regulate the money supply all over the country'.[6]

Recalling previous experiences in issuing banknotes, Pani recommended prudence and a law 'limiting the allowable maximum issue to just double the amount of gold held in cash in the metallic collateral of deposits – by providing that all notes would be issued only against domestic or foreign gold coins, or gold ingots at a rate of 75 centigrams of pure gold for each Peso'.[7] In fact, he suggested that the foundation of the Bank held 'a most relevant position within the framework of reconstruction, social reform and effort towards economic progress'.[8] However, the terrible experiences of the previous years made the government extremely cautious with respect to the issuing of banknotes.

The first note to be issued by the Bank of Mexico in 1925 was a 5 peso bill on which the portrait of a beautiful young woman in oriental attire is depicted in the centre, within a medallion, under the legend BANCO DE MEXICO (fig. 3). As had happened before, when popular expression called the 8 escudos coins (gold doubloons) 'peluconas' or 'wigged', because of the portrait of the king with an enormous wig, so this new note was in turn called the 'gitana' or 'Gypsy'. Mexicans then began to ask why an unknown girl should have been portrayed on the notes, and even the most illustrious numismatists embraced and published the generally accepted theory that the portrait was that of the mistress of the Finance Minister, Alberto J. Pani – a beautiful Catalonian artiste, Gloria Faure, who, along with her sister, another celebrated performer, delighted the capital's residents at that time. The story arose from the Minister's widespread reputation as a man of the world whose amorous adventures gave rise to much gossip concerning his philandering.

Antonio Deana Salmerón, a researcher whose works have enriched the Puebla Numismatic Society, made an erudite and precise description of the note, which reads as follows:

> Obverse – all of the decorative elements of the time are enclosed within a classical horizontal rectangle, overcharged with geometrical designs, with the number '5' placed at the four corners, inside irregular medallions. In the Centre, and towards the upper margin, arranged in a semicircle, and in two lines, the words 'El Banco de México'. Beneath an oval was the bust of a beautiful woman looking forward, wearing drop earrings and other pieces of jewellery according to the gypsy custom. A bead necklace adorned with coins fell from her forehead over her neck.

That is why, the researcher says, people began to call the notes *Billetes de la Gitana* (Gypsy banknotes). He continues to recount, in a second part, what helped to lay the foundation of the legend of the 5 peso note:

> It has been said that the famous theatrical performer, Gloria Faure, posed as the model for this note; that her picture appeared on that denomination for unexplained reasons. The voice of the people also says that this famous artist perhaps enjoyed the patronage of some high-ranking politician and that is why her

portrait was depicted on one of our bank notes. One thing we can be certain of is that while being popular on the stage, she became even more popular with the circulation of our five-peso note, her picture having been in the hands of almost every person from one end of the country to the other, from 1925 to 1970. During a 45-year period, we saw her image engraved on one of the most popular denominations of our money supply.[9] (fig. 4)

Don Alvaro J. Moreno's study on the effigies of women on Mexican banknotes takes note of this detail, expressing surprise that certain people who have nothing to do with the country's history should have been portrayed on its banknotes. In this respect, he wrote, 'This pretty lady's portrait, we know, is Gloria Faure's, a theatrical star living in Mexico on 1 September 1925, when the Banco de México, S. A. was established.'[10]

Without any doubt, the most joyful picture of this numismatic incident is provided by the distinguished Don Miguel L. Muñoz. He tells us, 'By that time [1925], two good-looking, popular Catalonian artists – the Faure sisters, Gloria and Laura – were in Mexico. Coincidentally, they needed to go to Europe. The most natural thing to do was, of course, to offer them transport in the Pullman to New York, so that they could embark to Europe. Since this would, obviously, make the trip much more pleasant for everybody, the necessary arrangements were made.'[11] In New York, they all stopped at the traditional Waldorf Astoria Hotel. While Pani devoted himself – not very successfully, indeed – to the economic negotiations aimed at modifying the Lamont-de la Huerta treaty to refund the Mexican debt, the Faure sisters visited the city. Although there was conflict between Pani and the US bankers over the debt arrangements, the New York press took a closer view of the Finance Minister's private life than of his official duties:

> One fine day, New Yorkers read in the press the report relating to the trip of Don Alberto in his private Pullman car and his attractive and endearing companions. Besides, the newspapers accused Mr Pani of having violated the principles established by the Republican Deputy for Illinois, Mr James Robert Mann, or the Mann Act, most commonly known as the 'White Slavery' Act. The police stormed Don Alberto's apartment thus creating a great scandal.[12]

Don Miguel adds still more details about the public official's New York adventure. One can verify the story's origin, not only from historical reports about Pani's well-earned fame, but also because Pani himself confirms the version very discreetly in his *Apuntes Autobiograficos*, where he added the note '*solo para mis hijos*' ('for my children only').[13] 'In January 1925, I was in New York for two weeks for informal talks with the American Chapter of the International Commission of Bankers with Businesses in Mexico. I prepared a memorandum where I asked that the "Lamont-de la Huerta" agreement be reviewed in order to limit the government's obligations to its actual financial capacity.'[14] From that moment on, says Pani:

> . . . a dreadful negotiation started together with copious correspondence. When the review had been accepted – excluding any modifications – I returned to New York only to meet with the bankers' resistance. The bankers' negative stance was

followed by a strange movement. Strange, indeed, because it was aimed at hampering negotiations. It is clear that I was not a saint but in spite of my philandering, I never disregarded my official duties. Besides, I also used the necessary discretion in order not to be disrespectful to my wife and children. A political enemy of mine, because of his de la Huerta sympathies, published or agreed to pose as the author of an article that appeared in the news, profiting from one of those 'indiscretions' which he exaggerated by adding a lot of novel lies with the purpose of accusing me of violating the 'Mann Act'. The New York press created a formidable scandal based on these statements. My room in the Waldorf Astoria hotel was searched by police who committed several other illegal acts. I was, however, not contacted personally. The scandal was echoed in most American newspapers, causing repercussions in Mexico, which provoked a stormy session at the Cámara de Diputados [the House of Representatives]. This ended in the appointment of a commission designated to ask President Calles to have me removed from office. With a view not to place the national decorum in a compromising situation due to resignation at the same time, President Calles kept his serenity as became his position. He laughed at the Deputies' prudishness and asked them – I was later told – whether they preferred a Presidential Cabinet consisting of eunuchs. He also telegraphed rejecting my resignation, and reiterating the confidence he had in me.[15]

President Calles' reaction was most understandable, for he could not do without such an able negotiator, and in fact a new agreement was finally signed with the Americans through the 'Enmienda Pani' or 'Pani Amendment', securing credit for Mexico. At the same time, General Calles apparently suffered from the same weakness with respect to the female sex as his Minister, and was even blamed for having obtained love tokens from Gloria Faure for himself, or so some journalist said: 'The [Banco de México] 5 peso note features a gypsy. A beautiful girl of impudent look and richly attired, an artist of the Mexican theatre by the name of Gloria Faure, charged with being the mistress of the President, Plutarco Elías Calles.'[16] It is quite possible that some chroniclers of the time could have confused the identity of the man. Evidently, however, Don Alberto J. Pani's forays gave scope for people to create a whole legend around these personages and, from very different standpoints, many people affirmed that 'the gypsy' on the 5 peso note was the Finance Minister's mistress. Don Miguel Muñoz considers this to be a 'numismatic revenge' against the Wall Street Boys, since 'a picture of Gloria Faure had been delivered opportunely to the American Bank Note Co. to serve as the model for the Banco de México, S. A., modern note vignette'. The legend grew. There were even those who thought it was the gesture of a romantic to immortalise his beloved.

Historical researchers, however, do not rest content with legends. Professor Guadalupe Monroy, who for many years was head of the Numismatic Museum of the Bank of Mexico wrote to the American Bank Note Company asking them for information on the origin of the effigy appearing on the 5 peso note. Her doubts were confirmed on 1 September 1976, when the answer arrived informing her that the effigy of that beautiful lady was but a stock vignette from their files, as is explained in the following letter:

> That beautiful lady's effigy was originally reproduced on September 27, 1910, on an engraving by Mr Robert Savage which was assigned number V43485 under the title 'the ideal head of an Algerian girl', having been kept among our vignette inventories to be used in the future. [illustration on p. 11]
>
> On April 1st, 1925, it was used for the first time on the five-peso note the initial order from Banco de México consisted of. On December 1933, Mr Sidney Smith engraved a miniature out of the same vignette which was identified under number V72982, having been placed among our inventories as well. It was used on the five-peso note ordered by the Banco de México on October, 1935 and in all the subsequent orders that we received from the Bank until 1970, when we printed the last five-peso note.

If the above letter was not enough to bring this persistent legend tumbling down, a series of trial note pieces made on behalf of the Mexican Republic Federal Government were discovered when the American Bank Note Company recently sold its files. The common obverse shows the national emblem, that is, the eagle facing front enclosed within a medallion, at the centre of the note. On the upper part is the legend GOBIERNO FEDERAL DE LA REPUBLICA MEXICANA (the Federal Government of the Republic of Mexico), in two lines; under the national emblem, the denomination is written in letters, VEINTE PESOS (twenty pesos) and underneath is the legend *La Tesorería de la Federación pagará al portador en efectivo el importe de este billete al constituirse las autoridades en la ciudad de México* (The Federal Treasury shall pay to the bearer in cash the amount of this note once the authorities are established in Mexico City). On each side of the emblem, with a guilloche pattern, is the denomination 20 in large numbers; underneath, in small characters, *Territorio Nacional* (National Territory) and on the other side, the date, 1 August 1915, which was to be signed by the Acting President and the Secretary of War. The number 20 is repeated in each corner. On the reverse, among guilloche drawings and two large figures of the number 20, we see before us the head of the famous gypsy (fig. 5) – much to our surprise, for this was ten years before the legend was born.

Notes

1. Venustiano Carranza (1859–1920) was a populist leader who opposed the conservative usurper Huerta. He was president from 1914 to 1920 and gave the country a new constitution in 1917.

2. Francisco Villa (1878–1923) also championed the rights of the people, and initially supported Carranza though he later turned against him.

3. Pani, Alberto J., *Apuntes Autobiograficos, Exclusivamente para mis hijos*, Mexico 1943, p. 179.

4. Ibid., p. 180.

5. Ibid., p. 315.

6. Ibid., p. 317.

7. Ibid., p. 318.

8. Carillo Flores, Antonio, 'Acontecimientos sobresalientes en la gestación y evolución del Banco de México', in Ernesto Fernández Hurtado, *Cincuenta anos de banca central, ensayos conmemorativos, 1925–1975*, Mexico 1976 (Lecturas 17), pp. 30–1.

9. Deana Salmerón, Antonio, *Los billetes de cinco pesos del Banco de México, S.A.*, Puebla 1976, pp. 17–18.

10. Moreno, Alvaro J., 'La Efigie de las damas en los billetes mexicanos', in *Memorias de la Academia Mexicana de Estudios Numismaticos*, Tomo II, enero-marzo 1971, no. 3, pp. 13–14.

11. Muñoz, Miguel, L., 'La gitana en los primeros billetes de cinco pesos del Banco de México, S.A.', in Sociedad Numismática de México, *Boletin*, vol. XII, Oct.–Nov. 1977, no. 97, pp. 129–30.

12. Ibid., pp. 130–1.

13. According to the information provided by his descendants, these memories were apparently written from notes that Don Alberto had dictated to one of his relatives.

14. Pani, op. cit., p. 332.

15. Pani, op. cit., p. 332–3.

16. Hidalgo Hernández, Alberto, 'Personajes que aparecen en el papel moneda de México', in Sociedad Numismática de México, *Boletin*, vol. XII, Jul.–Sept. 1978, no. 100, p. 91.

1 (*below*) Alberto J. Pani, founder of the Bank of Mexico, with President Calles during the bank's inauguration in 1925.

2 (*left*) The building of the Bank of Mexico, founded 'to issue money and regulate the money supply all over the country'.

3 The Bank of Mexico's first note, issued in 1925 and printed by the American Bank Note Company, was known as 'La Gitana' or 'The Gypsy'.

4 (below) The gypsy on the reduced size 5 peso note as it was issued by the Bank of Mexico from 1931 to 1972.

5 (bottom) Trial design for the 5 peso note, dated 1 August 1915, with, surprisingly, the head of the famous gypsy.

14

Soft images, hard currency: the portrayal of women on paper money

Virginia Hewitt

Paper money relies on public confidence. Whether it is issued by small private banks or central treasuries, in the turmoil of war or the optimism of a growing economy, the issuers will want their money to suggest 'good' qualities of financial stability and national wealth. Over and again, across centuries and continents, these desirable conditions have been embodied on notes by women – soft images to give hard currency a good name. The diversity of the designs is extraordinary, ranging from delicate nymphs giving decorative support to numerals or a bank's name, to powerful portraits of national figures. My aim in this article is to look at some of the questions raised by these images, by presenting not a straightforward chronology, but a thematic exploration of the ways women have been depicted on notes, and the insights this may give us into our perception of women and the role of currency design.[1]

The portrayal of women on paper money follows a well-established precedent, for female images have appeared on coins from early Greek issues to the present day. Nonetheless, given the tendency for women to be marginalised in terms of economic power, it is ironic that they have so often been chosen to bestow qualities of strength and power on to currency. Authoritative allegories abound on notes in the eighteenth and nineteenth centuries, when women had little public or private control over money,[2] and although many notes now carry portraits of renowned women, the position today may be less different than we would like to think. In many households the bank account is still the man's responsibility, and at the level of senior management, banking remains very much a male-dominated profession.[3] The first, fundamental question is therefore, why put images of women on notes at all?

Part of the answer may lie in the practice, stretching back to ancient civilisations, of using female figures as metaphors for other meanings and concepts, virtues and vices – though not surprisingly it is only the virtues we see on banknotes. Psychological theory has not yet played much, if any, part in numismatics, but it is clearly relevant to observe here that because of woman's biological role in child-bearing, female images are universal symbols of creation, an idea which may readily be ascribed to the creation of wealth. On paper money this is probably most often illustrated by women linked with symbols of agricultural fertility, but there are also designs which hint at deeper, more intuitive ideas of the feminine. Thus a German note of 1915 balances the alert figure of a male labourer, sleeve rolled up ready for work, with the serene image of a sleeping woman, her head bowed against the night sky – a contrast which reflects the symbolic association of man with daylight and reason, woman with the moon and mystery. It is striking, too, that many notes show women, especially allegorical figures, accompanied by animals. These are often lions, which undoubtedly are meant to suggest the strength and majesty of the state, but their presence also recalls the fact that in many mythologies female deities are depicted as animals, and that in many societies women themselves are equated with nature, the untamed. The provocative association of woman and animal, at once disturbing and empowering, is echoed in images such as that for a Brazilian note of 1907 on which a sulky personification of Law lounges against a sleeping lion, her arm dangling in its fur, or on notes from French Pacific colonies in the 1920s on which the huge heads of a bull and a tiger rest companionably on the thighs of an allegory of agriculture and a native woman, respectively (fig. 1). In yet other cases, as we shall see, female allegorical figures of authority are shown in ways which imply ambivalent attitudes towards the association of women with power.[4]

If this line of discussion seems to be straying into ambiguous and difficult territory, well, that is precisely the point. In the myth, legend and folklore of many cultures, images of women have long been used to embody abstract concepts, and those who issue and design paper money are no less subject to such influences than anyone else. Indeed their decisions will be bound by these unconscious factors, operating in conjunction with deliberate choices based on fashionable graphic design, available printing technology, and the type of information and image they want to project.

From the late seventeenth century until well into the nineteenth century these criteria were generally met by small black-and-white engravings on notes, intended to embellish the text, to deter forgery and to give the notes and their issuers a clear identity and authority. Many of the engravings were of neo-classical female allegorical figures, either as anonymous but alluring nymphs or, more often, as personifications of countries or institutions such as Law or Agriculture. So in Britain the Bank of England decorated its first notes in 1694 with a seated figure of Britannia, who has remained a feature of every Bank of England note to this day, while private banks throughout the country might choose a figure of Plenty or Agriculture to advertise the prosperity of local trade and, of course, the bank. It was also common to illustrate several of these positive concepts at once either by surrounding one figure with a rich array of attributes, or by grouping two or more different figures together.[5] Economic wealth is frequently implied by a single figure, often seated, surrounded by cog-wheels, agricultural implements and sheep, and packages ready for export on sailing ships viewed in the distance. In other circumstances, political power is the primary concern: one design on assignats issued during the French Revolution shows a female allegory holding fortune's rudder and a wreath of victory, and seated on a dais decorated with the cap of Liberty and *fasces* signifying authority (fig. 2). The interdependence of power and wealth is illustrated on a Canadian private note issue from Toronto in 1849, which in one vignette shows Britannia walking side-by-side with Justice, while in another she stands brandishing her spear and shield protectively above a grateful figure of Plenty, who sits beside a cornucopia spilling out coins (fig. 3). The differing positions of these figures seem to reflect the differing status of the two countries: Britain, the mother country, brings authority and just rule while Canada, the colony, offers her resources for material wealth. Another distinction is evident in their dress: the figure of state power, although female, wears masculine armour, but Plenty is softly draped in feminine robes. This easy association between femininity and fertility, and uneasy alliance between women and power, is evident on many note issues.

Neo-classical allegories have continued to appear on notes well into the twentieth century, sometimes to great effect. The beautiful helmeted head of a young Britannia introduced on the Bank of England's first coloured £5 note in 1957 has a timeless air of calm assurance, while on a note of Republican Spain in 1935 a haughty head of Tyche crowned with the city wall offers an imperious and appropriate alternative to a portrait of a monarch.[6] Other modern allegories may seem less apposite; in the Netherlands in 1921 a new note design juxtaposing a muscular blacksmith with an elegant Prosperity was mocked for its old-fashioned imagery. On the other hand, old and new may be happily combined, as on a delightful note issued in Ecuador during the 1940s to 1960s. Here a multi-talented allegory is endowed with classical robes, globe and scrolls – not to mention a pen and a telephone, connecting her to a city of skyscrapers in the distance (fig. 4).

The role played by modern allegories is not always so innocent, however. The European heritage of classical personifications is highly significant when they appear on colonial note issues of the 1930s and 1940s, often accompanied by a lifelike representation of an indigenous man or woman. Such images bridge traditional and modern elements of note design; they also reflect (or disguise) a collision of cultures. French colonial note issues in particular offer many dramatic visual variations on the theme of the allegorical personification of France leading and protecting the native peoples in her care. To give just one example, a striking French West African note of *c.* 1945 shows a white allegorical woman with her arm round the shoulders of a black indigenous woman, while the fingers of her other hand are entwined with those of the black woman's baby. Fantasy and reality, ruler and ruled, white and black are contrasted yet combined in unity.[7] There is, however, no doubt about who is in control, a fact more explicitly depicted on a Portuguese colonial issue for Angola at around the same time (fig. 5). Here again mother country and colony are represented by two women, but they are hardly sisters under the skin. The European figure of authority is an imaginary allegory, fully draped, giving guidance to the colony who is represented by a realistic figure of a native woman with naked breasts, kneeling in subservience beside her mentor. It is true that tenderness can be read into both the examples quoted, and no doubt these and similar notes were designed with the best of paternalist intentions – but the choice of images for the different meanings implicitly suppresses the status of blacks and real women, neither of whom are shown in positions of power.

It is also interesting that on colonial issues, allegories are always shown fully clothed, while their subjects are frequently semi-clad, although in other contexts – usually earlier note issues – allegorical women may well be shown with minimal (but strategic) covering. Given that note designs are intended to convey dignity, it is not surprising that they are seldom erotic,[8] and even partial nudity is generally reserved for scenes where it will not offend modesty, that is, for allegorical figures or non-European natives. The nude figures on Eliel Saarinen's designs for the Bank of Finland in the 1920s are an exception, but here too the aura of spiritual well-being is consistent with the symbolic meaning suggested by most nudity on notes – namely purity and integrity, or fertility and prosperity.[9] It should be pointed out, however, that whatever the possible subtexts of colonial issues, nudity in lifelike images of women need not be patronising, and can also be found on notes of independent countries: for example, a note issued in Swaziland in 1974 depicts a row of bare-breasted young women – the king's daughters no less – performing a ceremonial dance. Conversely, an intriguing inversion of practice is suggested by a recent newspaper article, reporting that Mali – once part of French West Africa, whose notes frequently depicted native women with exposed breasts – now will not accept Banque de France 100 franc notes because they reproduce the bare-breasted figure of Liberty from a famous painting.[10]

The symbolic association between a woman's breast and nourishment from a fertile nation is clear enough, but lifelike representations of women on banknotes usually make more indirect reference to their country's economic well-being. Vignettes on American notes of the nineteenth century provide early examples of designs equating a happy domestic and working life with the stable foundation of a bank in a local community,[11] but order and stability remain relevant for twentieth-century central banks and treasuries who want to promote the idea of a sound currency and a wealthy nation.

Scenes of women at home are unusual on notes, perhaps because the connotations are too personal for the broad canvas of a national currency; most frequently, women are shown working in key sectors of a country's economy, the cornsheafs and cog-wheels of earlier allegories now transformed into naturalistic views of fields and factories. The types of work shown are almost always traditional sources of female employment, such as harvesting roses in Bulgaria, coffee in Costa Rica or rice in Vietnam, manufacturing textiles in Albania or teaching children in South America or Africa. In at least one instance, the visual connection between women and traditional food provision was quite deliberate: the press release accompanying a new note issued in Zimbabwe in 1983 explained that the fruitful combination of progress and tradition was illustrated by showing modern fencing and cultivated fields next to women grinding maize in a traditional manner outside their huts (fig. 6).

The increasing use of more realistic images on notes during the twentieth century may be attributed to the larger scale of note-issuing institutions, more sophisticated printing technology, and the desire to replace outmoded neo-classical metaphors. Superficially, such scenes may seem to offer a more accurate depiction of women, but the implications remain complex. Firstly, however mundane the subject-matter of the design, the images themselves are usually marvellously idealised: a woman in Mali picks cotton as though it were a rose, a young woman in communist China drives a tractor and lets her short hair blow freely in the heady breeze of sexual equality . . . (fig. 7). It is hard to believe that the reality of either economic conditions or most women's lives often conforms to these glamorous pictures. Secondly, despite their romantic glow, the apparently straightforward narrative content of such note designs disguises the fact that the women portrayed are still symbols of economic growth, national wealth or cultural identity. A Swiss note design of 1923 is a case in point: a peaceful interior scene shows three women embroidering one cloth. They probably represent the harmonious co-operation of the three distinct communities who formed the original Confederation, but what do we see? Three women sewing quietly at home (fig. 8). There seems to be a catch, however we look at these images, for taken at face value they perpetuate conventional and limited views of woman's role and yet, taken as symbols, they elevate menial work to a higher plane.

For many people the most familiar images of women on banknotes are portraits. Once again, these are not a new element of note design: although Bank of England notes did not feature a portrait of the monarch until 1960, charming vignettes of Queen Victoria are found on local British notes and colonial issues in the nineteenth century. American notes of this period also carried occasional portraits of contemporary women who were not heads of state – but they usually had good connections. Notes issued by the Confederate States were graced by a pretty profile of Lucy Holcombe Pickens, a woman admired for her beauty, virtue and strong character; she was thus the very essence of the best Southern qualities and also, significantly, the wife of the governor of South Carolina.[12] However, it is in the second half of the twentieth century that portraits have become a standard component of note design. This has much to do with the practical function of a fine engraving in deterring forgery and generating fast recognition of different notes – faces quickly catch our attention. But portraits may also appeal because they relate to the modern world's approval of individual attainment, and bring personality to notes which are now issued by vast and impersonal institutions. Indeed it is clear that the public expect to recognise the figures portrayed on their notes, judging by the bemused reaction to the Bank of England £50 note issued in 1994, its tercentenary year, featuring Sir John Houblon, the Bank's first governor. He may be a key player in the Bank's history, but the general public have never heard of him.[13]

Of all human images on notes, portraits should have the greatest capacity to convey individual character and a sense of reality. Portraits of Golda Meir (former prime minister, on notes of Israel in the 1980s) (fig. 9), Maria Montessori (founder of the educational system, on notes of Italy in the 1990s) or Selma Lagerlöf (Nobel prize-winner for literature, on notes of Sweden in the 1990s) are all appealing images of real and indeed older women, which offer much more than mere ornament. Yet the fact remains that even such women still appear as symbols, their personal status translated into public glory. As with other aspects of designs on paper money, portraits must comply with the desired impression of national strength and dignity, and this will inevitably affect the choice of people to be portrayed. Apart from monarchs or heads of state, who appear by virtue of their office, they are almost always historical figures, who may perhaps have been pioneers in their time, but are now safely absorbed into their country's heritage. Among portraits of women, other interesting patterns emerge. It is true that many countries now deliberately choose to depict women as well as men on their paper money, and it is also true that the women shown often achieved recognition in professions which are also practised by men. But pursuing the tendency in the naturalistic scenes of women at work, portraits tend to focus on stereotypically female occupations. The arts, especially literature, are well represented by women, perhaps because art rather than science is easily identified with particular cultures, but also presumably because there have traditionally been fewer opportunities for women in the fields of science and technology. It is surely significant too that many of the women depicted are honoured for their work in human welfare. An interesting choice is made on a Portuguese note of 1960, portraying Isabel, who was queen in the late thirteenth and early fourteenth centuries and was made a saint in 1626 for her life of prayer and good works, including the provision of care for 'fallen' women. More recently, a familiar and popular Bank of England note featured Florence Nightingale, who reformed the appalling barracks hospital at Scutari during the Crimean War, and later established standards of nursing education in Britain, while Australia has portrayed Dame Mary Gilmore, a poet and active campaigner against injustice towards the poor and disadvantaged – including women.[14] To do such work, all these women must have kicked hard against the prevailing customs and systems of their times, but now it may be wondered whether in appearing on national currencies they are being honoured as much for rebellion as for tenderness and compassion, conventionally regarded as feminine traits. In this sense these portraits may be seen as modern embodiments of the high virtues personified in earlier allegorical forms.

In this paper I have focused on some dominant themes in the imagery of women on paper money, and offered an unashamedly conjectural analysis of how these may be interpreted: indeed, the thrust of my argument is that designs on notes contain far more than the factual content which meets the eye. Such an approach offers the possibility of widening our understanding in several areas. Firstly, there are obviously implications for how we perceive women. This is rarely a consideration in the choice of note designs, but it is part of their legacy. I am not suggesting that the ways in which women are portrayed on notes are always or necessarily wrong, merely that they represent and reinforce ambivalent and partial truths about the reality of woman's place in different societies. The images reflect conventional assumptions, which then gain apparent validity from the official nature of money, mass-produced for millions to use.

Secondly, there is a point here about numismatic study. Traditionally, and with good reason, this has tended to concentrate heavily on how and why money is issued, and to pay less attention to its psychological impact. Essentially money is made for people to use – so we may ask what part does it play in their everyday lives, what do they think about it, what does it say about them? Just because it is hard to answer such questions does not mean that they should not be asked.

Finally, there is the broad question of design, symbolism and perception. Money is a powerful, unsuspected vehicle for official advertisement and propaganda, passing on both consciously chosen ideas and unconscious assumptions. Authorities will choose designs to promote the public image they wish to create, yet to achieve this effect, that image must be acceptable and recognisable to the public. To some extent, therefore, note designs show us ourselves as we wish to be seen. It has been argued that such considerations are of little importance, because no one really looks at money, and most people cannot easily name even the famous figures on the notes of their own country. But we all know how to tell one note from another; subliminally we do recognise the designs on our notes. The images and their mixed meanings are there, and if we think that we do not see them, that only makes them matter all the more.

Notes

1. For a fuller discussion of the subject, see Virginia Hewitt, *Beauty and the Banknote: Images of Women on Paper Money*, London 1994.
2. See Richard G. Doty's article, 'Surviving images, forgotten peoples', in this volume, for a discussion of how women and other groups outside the money economy are depicted on United States obsolete notes.
3. For example, the first woman was appointed to the Court of Directors of the Bank of England as recently as 1993.
4. See Marina Warner, *Monuments and Maidens. The Allegory of the Female Form*, London 1987, for an analysis of female images as metaphor; M. Esther Harding, *Woman's Mysteries*, London 1991, for a psychological interpretation of the feminine principle in myth and folklore; and Anne Baring and Jules Cashford, *The Myth of the Goddess. Evolution of an Image*, London 1993, for an account of goddess religions and their significance. In *Managing Monsters: Six Myths of Our Time, The Reith Lectures 1994*, London 1994, Marina Warner explores ways in which myth is still manifested and created in everyday life.

   An interesting earlier example of ambiguous undercurrents in female personifications of money is found in an anonymous sixteenth-century poem in 'prayse of Lady Pecunia' (kindly brought to my

attention by my colleague Barrie Cook). It is pointedly addressed 'To the Gentleman Readers', and although the author grants it is useless to withstand this lady's powers, these are described not only in terms of wealth, but also in language full of sexual innuendo.

5. Groups of figures may also be used to represent commercial or political co-operation between different countries, either as equal partners or in a colonial relationship, as discussed later in this article.
6. See Teresa Tortella's article in this volume regarding the deliberate change of designs on Spanish Republican note issues.
7. I have recently seen a powerful echo of this image in a current prospectus for a British girls' school, in which racial harmony is implied by a photograph of two pupils, white and black, shown side by side, the fair-haired white girl with her arm around the black girl's shoulder.
8. Although public imagination may invest the most innocent images with sensual overtones; see Elsa Lizalde Chavez' article in this volume.
9. See Tuukka Talvio's article in this volume for a discussion of the ideological content of Saarinen's designs.
10. The *Observer*, 17 April 1994. My thanks to Douglas Anderson for pointing this out. The painting in question is *La Liberté guidant le peuple*, 1830, by Eugène Delacroix.

11. See Richard G. Doty in this volume, and Francine Tyler, 'The Angel in the Factory: Images of Women Workers Engraved on Ante-Bellum Bank notes', in *Imprint. Journal of the American Historical Print Collectors Society*, vol. 19, no. 1, Fairfield, Connecticut, Spring 1994.
12. See Guy R. Swanson's article in this volume, fig. 5.
13. Criticism that this choice was self-congratulatory is consistent with more general complaints in Britain that the high street banks tend to be indifferent to their customers'

needs. In response, the banks now compete with each other in advertising more direct and personal attention.
14. The life of the woman featured on the most recent Australian issue, a $20 note brought out in 1993, presents a varied profile. Mary Reibey (1777–1855) arrived in Australia as a convict, but through her marriage became a wealthy and successful businesswoman. However, it is presumably also significant that she was well respected for her involvement with charities, the church and education.

1 Female figures with a bull and a tiger on a 100 franc note of Tahiti, 1920.

2 Allegorical female figure with symbols of freedom, victory and authority on a 50 livres note of France, 1792.

3 Britannia protecting a seated figure of Plenty on a $5 note of the Farmer's Joint Stock Bank, Toronto, Canada, 1849.

4 Allegorical woman with classical and modern attributes
   on a 1,000 sucres note of Ecuador, 1940s–60s.

5 Native woman and western
   allegorical figure on a 5 angolares
   note of Angola, 1947.

6 Women grinding maize on a $5 note of Zimbabwe, 1983.

7 Young woman with windswept hair driving a tractor on a 1 yuan note of the People's Bank of China, 1960.

8 Three women embroidering one cloth on a 500 franc note of Switzerland, 1923.

9 Golda Meir, prime minister of Israel from 1969 to 1974, on a 10 new sheqalim note of the Bank of Israel, 1985.

Index